Supporting Deaf Children and Young People

Also available from Continuum

Special Educational Needs, Mary Warnock, Brahm Norwich and Lorella Terzi
Supporting Children with Learning Difficulties, Christine Turner

Supporting Deaf Children and Young People
Strategies for Intervention, Inclusion and Improvement

Derek Brinkley

Supporting Children

continuum

Continuum International Publishing Group

The Tower Building
11 York Road
London SE1 7NX

80 Maiden Lane
Suite 704
New York NY 10038

www.continuumbooks.com

British Library Cataloguing-in-Publication Data
A catalogue record for this book is available from the British Library.

ISBN: 978-1-4411-5359-3 (paperback)

Library of Congress Cataloging-in-Publication Data
A catalog record for this book is available from the Library of Congress.

Typeset by Newgen Imaging Systems Pvt Ltd, Chennai, India
Printed and bound in India

To the late Dr. Terry Morris
who gave me my first chance in Deaf education,
to Kate Murray who gave me my last
and to Collette Eales whose idea this was

Contents

Preface

There are two types of books about Deaf Education: those written by Deaf people and those written by hearing people. This is one of the latter.

There are two types of books about Deaf Education: those written by oralists and those written by signers. This is one of the latter.

Nonetheless, I hope that much of what I have to say is relevant to all those involved in Deaf Education, in whatever capacity and whatever situation.

A few years ago I might have begun by saying, 'There are two types of books about Deaf Education: those written for people working in Schools for the Deaf and those written for people working in mainstream schools.' The former are now an endangered species and any author who writes solely for them is destined to starve on the embankment in company with those bridge players who neglected to draw trumps. After many years in a School for the Deaf, I worked for 6 years in a mainstream school, sometimes teaching discrete groups of Deaf students, sometimes supporting individuals or small groups in mainstream classes. In this book I have not always tried to distinguish which of these last two contexts I am dealing with, since I think most is applicable to both. Those who work exclusively in one context will therefore not be able to claim a reduction in the price of the volume, but they receive my personal apology for forcing them to read the lot!

I have used the capitalized Deaf to refer to those who belong to and identify with or may at some point aspire to join the social community of the Deaf. I have used the uncapitalized deaf to refer to a simple medical diagnosis of hearing loss. And in the anecdote about the deaf dog!

Descriptions of BSL signs are based on the north-east of England model. Readers living elsewhere may need to make slight adjustments.

This book is not a set of ipse dixits which you must follow. But I hope that it contains good advice. Even more, I hope there is material here which is both controversial and thought-provoking enough to help you examine how you work with the Deaf. Because there are two types of books about Deaf Education: those which make you think and . . .

Introduction

Introduction

Introduction

This is a chapter I would prefer not to write. I would much rather dive into the middle of the really useful stuff. I am acutely aware that those who pick up a novel and find that the opening sentence is 'It was a dark and stormy night' are likely to throw it away and go off in search of a Tom Clancy instead. Likewise, I am sure that there is a temptation when faced with pages full of introductory information on the Deaf to abandon the whole book and go off in search of the Deaf Educator's equivalent of Tom Clancy, whoever that may be. Perhaps Nolan. Perhaps Tucker.

However, I am also anxious not to appear like one of those computer wizards who when you ask them a simple question run their fingers over the keyboard so quickly that the plastic starts to melt, while reciting so much jargon that you begin to wonder if even the word 'and' is being used in a specialized way.

So here is my equivalent of the Frequently Asked Questions (FAQ) feature that you can find and ignore on most good websites.

But before I begin, an important word of warning. You may begin to read this and think, 'That's a bit of a simplification.' You will be wrong. It will in fact be a gross, massive oversimplification and generalization! Nearly everything I say should be prefixed by the words 'Generally speaking, but with many exceptions because individual Deaf students are very different, ...' The wonders of copy and paste do actually make it possible to append this note to every single comment I make in the book, with little hardship to myself. But in the interests of your sanity I have decided not to – on condition you bear these words constantly in mind.

What do Deaf people actually hear?

This is probably the question that crops up most. It is endlessly fascinating because for very different reasons neither Deaf nor hearing people are able to answer it accurately.

The first advice is to listen to how they speak. Many Deaf, particularly those who are especially well motivated towards oral communication, or have been very well drilled in it, will speak considerably better than they hear; but few are perverse enough to deliberately speak worse than they hear.

However immediately lose the notion, if you ever had it, that what the Deaf hear is what the hearing hear, only much quieter. If that were so, hearing aids and shouting would solve the problem, and in most cases they do not. This 'flat loss' is rare in children with a severe or profound hearing loss.

Much more common is the 'ski slope', so called because their audiograms show hearing in the very low frequencies, but swiftly plummet down between 500–1,000 Hz before disappearing off the map by 4,000 Hz. This kind of loss gives access to the vowel sounds but comparatively little to the consonants. Hence, in very simplified terms they could be expected to hear something along the lines of a a i e u e i o e a ai o a–e. If this is amplified, the result is not something close to normal speech, but only A A I E U E I O E A AI O A–E; this is not greatly helpful, and explains why shouting at the Deaf is not often successful.

The reverse ski slope, where they hear mainly consonants rather than vowels, is possible, but rare, and less of a problem. If faced with Jck nd Jll wnt p th hll t ftch pl f wtr, you could probably make a guess at the meaning without having to meld in the vowels from the preceding paragraph.

All this ignores the fact that there are lots of other noises going on in the frequencies where they have hearing and it is very difficult for them to distinguish between wanted and unwanted sounds. Modern hearing aids claim to amplify only the speech sounds and filter out the noise; but even if they are successful in this, many Deaf claim to have noises in their head, which come as part of the package of damage to the hearing system. In spite of a number of book titles, what the Deaf hear is rarely silence.

Why are people deaf?

If all the deaf people from the local area were to be brought together in one place, what would be most immediately noticeable would be the high age profile. Most deafness is the result of the ears joining in the general deterioration of the body parts that comes with age. No doubt, as those who in their youth have abused their sense of hearing with the aid of speakers at discos and nightclubs move into middle age, the average will come down a little. But none of these are the deaf that concern the readers of this book.

The crowd might also include the unilaterally deaf – those deaf in only one ear. Diseases such as measles and mumps can cause deafness, but you need to be exceptionally unlucky for it to affect both ears. Also those who permanently damage one ear by poking something into it tend to learn the lesson quickly enough to avoid wasting the other one as well. The deafness on one side may make them irritable, or indeed irritating, but to us as teachers they are rarely our concern either.

Then there are the adventitiously deaf – those who suddenly went deaf as the result of a fall, car crash or some similar trauma.

This large group might even include all those who have middle ear effusion (otitis media) or as they, somewhat optimistically, will put it, 'are a bit bunged up with a cold'. Since these are mostly children, you may occasionally be asked to give advice to or about them; but they too are not your staple diet.

So there remains a small minority who are your main customers – those who have been bilaterally severely/pro-foundly deaf from an early age: what the Deaf themselves tend to refer to as the Born Deaf, although illnesses in the first 4 years or so, of which meningitis is the most common, lead to the same problem – namely deafness before language has been acquired.

The national programme of inoculation has more or less wiped out rubella in pregnancy as a major cause of deafness, and with it has gone the battery of eyesight problems, emotional spasms and physical lack of control of the limbs that so often accompanied these cases. Other viral conditions of the mother around the tenth to twelfth week of pregnancy, when the ear is beginning to develop, such as Cytomegalovirus (CMV), continue to cause deafness, but their lack of symptoms at the time often hide the fact that they are the cause. Moreover, what medical science gives with one hand it takes away with the other, because as rubella has declined, the number of children surviving premature or traumatic birth has increased, leading to many cases of deafness, and often other accompanying physical, mental and emotional problems.

Vast numbers of cases of deafness simply go down as unknown. A lot of these are probably genetic, but there again some of those which go down as genetic may well be unknown. Here's how it works.

Doctor (to mother of child recently diagnosed as deaf): Any problems during birth?

Mother: No.

Doctor: Any illness during the first 3 months of pregnancy?

Mother: No. [As already mentioned, this will not track down causes like CMV, which often display no symptoms, or just a mild 'under the weather' feeling that no woman is going to remember a couple of years later.]

Doctor: Any deafness in the family?

Mother: There's Aunty Edith.

And so the doctor, who was just about to write unknown since he had run out of questions, happily writes genetic. Of course, he might have gone on to ask, 'Is that the Edith who's 84, worked as a steel hammerer during the war and went deaf two years ago?'

It is to be hoped that with so many health trusts now having in place early testing/diagnosis schemes, allied with equally early intervention from trained audiologists, this kind of interview is becoming rarer. It is to be hoped!

Why don't doctors cure them?

There are basically two kinds of deafness: conductive and sensory-neural.

Think of sound as a car trying to drive to your brain. With a conductive loss you are in a London street at rush hour with road works going on. The hearing system is clogged up. You have wax, a split eardrum, infection in the middle ear, mastoid problems and the tiny bones in your ossicular chain have broken and become detached. Things are not looking good, but a doctor on point duty will come along and there is every chance that things can be sorted out.

With a sensory-neural loss you are in Beirut and someone has bombed the road. The cochlea, which converts the sound to tiny electrical impulses that the brain can understand, is hardly working at all. This is the cause of most severe and profound deafness. Twenty years ago there was no cure. Full stop. In recent years there have been cochlear implants – effectively an electronic artificial cochlea. These are discussed later in the book, but they tend to be more successful with people who have gone deaf later in life and who have already experienced speech.

Why can't they just lip-read?

Some of us were brought up on detective stories that either began or ended with a Deaf person looking through a pair of binoculars into the hotel room opposite, and lip-reading one of the gang saying, 'So, Fat Tony, we hold up the Chase Manhattan Bank on Fourth Street at 10.07 next Tuesday.' In fact, lip-reading is exceedingly difficult for anyone, particularly for the Deaf. Many quite distinct words look identical on the lips. Also – and the Deaf are greatly inconvenienced by this – it is difficult to lip-read without a good understanding of the structure of English, which gives so many clues as to what words to expect and which of the indistinguishables is more likely. Not to have this basis is a bit like trying to do a cryptic crossword in a foreign language; you lack the clues that you yourself bring to the puzzle from your experience of the ambiguities of English wording.

Finally, context is all-important. If you walk up to a Deaf student and ask, 'What is your name? How old are you?' you are likely to be told, 'I'm John Smith and I'm thirteen.' You will reflect on what a good lip-reader he is. But try asking, 'Where is your gnome? How cold are you?' and you are likely to get the same answer, rather than the hoped-for information 'It's in the rockery and I'm freezing' – *unless* you have just been discussing garden ornaments and the breakdown of the school heating system.

Lip-reading is useful in social contexts where you can predict the general flow of the conversation. It is a different matter in a Biology lesson discussing the life cycle of the Mexican boll weevil.

What should I remember when trying to communicate with the Deaf?

All openings to books like this contain a list of dos and don'ts for good communication. These are deeply worthy, and each is in its own way, and in the right context, correct. The problem is that they are so often presented as if they are all and always of equal and supreme importance, for example:

- Don't sport a beard and/or moustache. The theory of this is that it makes you more difficult to lip-read. I suspect that in reality it is just that the traces of yesterday's breakfast are distracting.
- Don't wear bright-coloured or highly decorated clothing above the waist; it gives your signing space the equivalent of glare from a television screen.
- Catch the attention of the Deaf by switching a light on and off. This works quite well if you have a large roomful of mainly Deaf students all engaged in some activity. But I have seen people do it in a classroom where to reach the light switch they had to walk past the only two Deaf in the room and could perfectly well have simply tapped on the desk they were working at.

- Don't stand with your back to a window. In theory the dazzling light from outside shadows your face making lip-reading difficult. In practice, every school I have ever worked in has such vast candlepower in their lighting system that even a comparatively bright British day outside will have little effect on it.

- Don't shout. This is good advice if you are having difficulty making yourself understood. But if you are angry at a student who has just done something that is both stupid and dangerous – shout. The sound and the resultant facial expression and body language will successfully remove any ambiguities about your opinion of their deed.

- Don't speak unnaturally loudly, slowly or deliberately. This distorts both sound and lip pattern.

- Get the person's attention first. Waving a hand in their peripheral vision is the approved method. Tapping them on the shoulder from behind and making them jump out of their skin is effective, but unlikely to win you a cooperative audience.

- Whatever your strategy in Ibiza when foreigners don't understand you, if the Deaf look puzzled at what you have said/signed, try to remould the sentence into a simpler form, rather than repeating the original rather slower and louder/bigger.

If you understand why the last three bits of advice above are a hundred times more important than the first three, your communication with the Deaf will rapidly improve.

1

Language

Language acquisition

In the heady days of the militancy of the National Union of the Deaf, one of their most frequently enunciated slogans was that the Deaf are not disabled, they are a language minority.

It is easy to pass over this by saying, 'Right! But they are still keen enough to claim all the financial benefits that go to groups of Disabled.' It is easy to argue that simply declaring they would have no problems if only everything were available in British Sign Language (BSL) is wholly impractical since society cannot afford to featherbed such a small minority. It is easy to point out the everyday problems from traffic awareness to several people speaking at once, which are not solvable in simply language terms. And yet there is an essential truth underlying that statement which passes over the heads of so many hearing people: that the biggest problem faced by the Deaf is not that they cannot hear, but that they cannot acquire language in the way that the majority do, which is the most efficient way.

I doubt if many people would relish suddenly being asked to give an impromptu lecture on audiology to a group of French students who have no knowledge of English, relying solely on what they can recall from their schoolday French and the occasional phrasebook before setting out on holiday. They would find both their vocabulary and their grammatical expression confined to what they had been formally taught, as opposed to English where they continually learn, revise and reinforce their language skills by what they overhear, from television to the supermarket queue. Not only would they lack knowledge of what to say, they would be hesitant and embarrassed at their inadequacy.

Yet this is in effect the situation in which most Deaf students find themselves most of the time in school. They are expected to be educated and communicate in a language that they are still in the early stages of learning rather than in one they have long since acquired. This is true whether their language is BSL or English. Even those (and they are very much a minority) who are Deaf children of Deaf parents, though they will probably be exposed to good quality signing at home, will still not be exposed, in the world outside the home or via television/radio/music within the home, to the range and frequency of language which most hearing children receive.

In most homes with a Deaf child who requires signing, only the most direct conversation with the child is signed. Even when both parents are learning to sign (and it is frightening how often this is regarded as the job only of the mother; though not as frightening as those fortunately rare cases where neither parent learns to sign so that the child's preschool communication is no more than just a bit of pointing) they rarely conduct their household business and their day-to-day chat accompanied by sign. And even were they to do so, in contrast to sound which is taken in by the hearing even when their eyes are elsewhere, signing has to be watched; if the child is looking elsewhere the signing will go unnoticed. The very fact that the parents are in most cases (the exception is likely to be where there is already an older Deaf child in the family) learning signing from scratch is liable to mean that the sign input they give will tend to be a simple matter of pointing to things and signing a word or two. Those who are familiar with the use of Makaton among hearing children with severe learning difficulties will understand what I mean. But of course Deaf children do not have those learning difficulties and ideally require as full and structured a language as possible.

Teaching language to the Deaf

Having now made that charge against parents, who are doing their best in difficult circumstances and with little knowledge/experience, it is an unpleasant but necessary duty to ask the question: to what extent do teachers do the same? Do they offer Deaf students a full language experience, as opposed to just a vocabulary?

Of course, in practical terms, there are times when it is necessary to cut language to the minimum to ensure communication. One of the best conversations I ever heard involved a teacher telling a student that the temporary classroom they usually used for their lesson was out of bounds due to an examination:

> **Teacher:** We can't use the hut today because there is an exam going on in there. So we'll find somewhere else.
> **Student:** What?
> **T:** Today there is an examination in the hut. We cannot use it. We must find another room instead.
> **S:** What?
> **T:** Before we use hut. Today exam in hut. We cannot use hut because of exam. We use different room.
> **S:** What?
> **T:** Look – TODAY NOTHING HUT!
> **S:** Ah! OK. Today nothing hut!

But day in and day out you should be looking for opportunities to present a structure of language.

I once worked in a school in which for a while we attempted to use, at least in the context of teaching English, a system of Signed English, with 'markers' to show regular and irregular plurals, varieties of tense and so on, and a host of invented signs for words such as *if*, *the*, *so* and *and*. I am sure that some would make the accusation against us that we had already sold the pass to the Persians when we made the provision 'at least in the context of teaching English'. We tended to justify ourselves by saying things like, 'In a lot of what we do, for ease and speed of communication we use Sign Supporting English (SSE), but if we want to give exact dictation of notes, or are helping them to write an essay, we can shift into Signed English.'

We eventually abandoned the Signed English. Partly it was through opposition from the local Deaf, who were finding that some of our students and ex-students who went into the Deaf Clubs were almost incomprehensible to most of the members because of the strange extras they were throwing into their signing. But also there was little if any evidence that the process was improving the grammar and syntax of their English. I understand that there is a strong argument that the reason our Signed English didn't work is that we did not show 100 per cent commitment to it for long enough. If only we had used it all day, in and out of class, and persuaded parents to do the same, it might have worked. Or it might not, and our students, like those elsewhere who used Paget-Gorman (an artificial sign system used mainly in certain schools in Scotland), might have ended up with an ability to sign in school but not in the Deaf world they were going into. When I taught the hearing, I had a wonderful student who comprehended all lessons really well, but whose spelling was so atroshus that he almost failed to get into Yewneeversytee. He had originally gone to a school that used Initial Teaching Alphabet (ITA), then moved to one that didn't and spent the rest of his life in a kind of spelling limbo. This can just as well happen to our students' signing if we put up artificial barriers to easy communication with the rest of the Deaf world.

But to go back to our attempts at Signed English, the reason some of us became disillusioned with it is that we became conscious that grammar and syntax were not the be all and end all of language. It seemed far more important to have fluid conversations in which students could build up the most basic language skill, which is to achieve the flexibility of word/sign manipulation that allows clear communication (externally) and thought patterns (internally).

Problems of language acquisition

To return belatedly to the analogy of being educated in a foreign language, this is, if anything, a gross underestimation of the problem suffered by the Deaf. Most spoken languages are to a greater or lesser extent tied to their written form by phonetic links. Therefore, even taking into account Shaw's strictures on the irregularities of English spelling/pronunciation, if you are a native speaker of English and I say a word you have never come across before, there is a good chance that you can write it down, if not wholly accurately, at least closely enough for another English speaker to recognize it. Conversely, if you see a word you have never heard written down, you could probably make a reasonable attempt to pronounce it. If the word is in French or German or Welsh it is much harder. It might illuminate this point a little to quote a story told by the Welsh painter Kyffin Williams about two Englishmen who visited Llanfairpwllgwyngyllgogerychwyrndrobwllllantysiliogogogoch. They stared in awe at the name on the railway station but had no idea how to read it, so they went to get something to eat in a nearby establishment where they had the following conversation with the Welsh lady serving:

TE: What do you call this place?

WLS: What do mean? It's written up.

TE: Yes but we can't say it.

WLS: You say it just how it's written.

TE: I'm afraid that doesn't work for us. You see, we're English.

WLS: Ah, English, is it? Alright. I'll help you then. We say it: Bur-Ger-King!

Of course, as you began to learn the language it would become easier. But think of the difficulty if the language were traditional Mandarin Chinese, where there is absolutely no link between the sound of the word and the pictogram that represents it. This is precisely the relationship between English and sign. If you have never seen the word 'Irish' written down but were told you had to write it you might spell it Eyerish. It would cause momentary confusion, but no insuperable problem, because it is based on phonetics. But if your only experience of the word 'Irish' is a middle finger on the right hand flicking the left shoulder, and you are told to write it down, you have no starting point whatsoever.

Just to make things even worse, if you make use of lip-reading, but do not have enough hearing to establish a bond between phonics and lip shape, you are left with yet another completely disparate set of shapes to learn by heart – lip pattern as well as sign and written/finger-spelt letters.

The plateau of Deaf English

The fact remains, and has remained with us for a long time now, that though there are a number of honourable exceptions, not only do Deaf students lag well behind the literacy ability that would be expected of their hearing contemporaries, but also when they reach a reading age of about 8½ they are unlikely to make significant improvement on that figure for a considerable period – often not for as long as they are in school. This is the dreaded plateau.

Of course there is one sense in which this is an illusion. The students do not, for example, stop increasing their vocabulary. In fact, as they do more academic work the technical vocabulary grows exponentially. But vocabulary is not the same as language. Whether urban myth or not, there is a story that some years ago some academics ran a Fog test (test of readability level) on sample pages of two books and came to the conclusion that Bill Naughton's *The Goalkeeper's Revenge*, a popular book with young boys, was much harder to read than the other. The other happened to be Wittgenstein's *Tractatus Logico-Philosophicus*. The Fog test takes much account of the length and complexity of vocabulary. Wittgenstein went on at great length along the lines of 'If things that are are and things that are not are not, can we say that things that are not are because what they are is that they are being things that are not?' To be honest, I made that sentence up. But the point is valid. There is nothing in that sentence that children could not 'read', though I doubt if it would make much sense to them. Deaf students often 'bark at print'; that is, they sign or pronounce the individual words on the page but do not process them so that they take in the actual meaning. Another strategy, when a signer is reading, is for them simply to grunt, finger spell the initial letter and pass on swiftly to the next word, hoping we won't ask questions.

Once the plateau is reached, Deaf students then face the problem of the dichotomy between information and the carrier language. The texts written for children with a reading age of 8½ are likely to be aimed at children of a similar chronological age. Once you get well beyond that age you no longer want to read about such 'babyish' things. But books or magazines dealing with the football, or fashion, which you are interested in, are too hard to read; so you stop reading except in school when you have to; and so your reading level shows no improvement. This is not just a problem for the Deaf, but it is especially a problem for the Deaf given that they are often already alienated and/or limited by the lack of relevance to Deaf life and culture in most of what is available for them to read.

Strategies to improve literacy standards in Deaf students – reading

I have emphasized the importance of the Deaf Literacy Problem. It is very tempting to sign off by saying, 'If you complain that I have not outlined a solution, I can only say that if I had the solution I would have retired years ago. If I have helped clarify the problem, my job is done.' But since this rather savours of showing a drowning man a PowerPoint on the history of swimming, I will make a few suggestions, which, if they do not constitute a guaranteed lifebelt, may at least give you a piece of wreckage to cling onto.

The first thing, the most important thing, indeed the sine qua non, is that you must first give the child language. Whether that language is English, BSL or something else does not matter. The child must have inside them the realization that a language is a pattern of concepts that allow them to communicate meaningfully and originally – not pointing, not miming, not echolalic imitation, but creative language. Once they have that proficiency they can move on to literacy. If this seems too obvious please bear in mind that there are families in which this kind of language experience is not offered to Deaf children (arguably not to hearing children either). However, while professionals are busy tut-tutting at the inadequacy of feckless parents, let no one forget that we are not too far from a time when schools saw articulation as being the most important element of communication.

In any conversation I have about literacy, I want to begin with enjoyment. If the Good Wish Fairy offered to give our children pleasure in reading, or an English scheme of work in line with most recent curriculum requirements and a subject leader fully familiar with national expectations, I might try to schmooze her to give me both, but I know which one I would settle for.

The primary aim has to be to make reading attractive to the children, because only when they have begun to read avidly will they have the experience of English which will enable their writing to develop. It would be nice if they were surrounded at home and in the community by books and other opportunities to read, along with the sight of adults reading, and enjoying and encouraging that reading. School staff cannot guarantee that. But they can create that atmosphere for the time the students are in school – by displays, by the resources that are made available, by the time that the students are given to use the resources and by the staff's own attitude to books – and indeed to other text – because reading from an internet page is as legitimate a reading experience as *War and Peace* (and usually a bit shorter).

If they are not reading for pure pleasure they should be reading for relevance. This is cross-curricular English because this is what those teaching the Deaf should do all the time in their lessons – give students really exciting and interesting lessons incorporating texts that they want to read because they are relevant.

Schools need to create additional reading time for Deaf students; not reading lessons, but break/lunch/after school opportunities to sit around reading, by themselves or with friends, with a teacher/learning support assistant (LSA) who can help if they need it but who is not enforcing, checking or interfering. And the adult should of course not be supervising, but deeply engaged in reading!

The time, the space, the adult are all quite easy to provide; but what are much harder to supply are the actual resources. Resources must be age appropriate, relevant to the students' lives, real or aspirational, and above all enjoyable. And if this isn't hard enough, they must be frequently changed or at least supplemented. Books like this are hard to find; but please note I have been using the word 'resources' not 'books'. Resources can be comics, magazines, web pages (hard copy or on screen), newsletters or advertising material; although I was lucky enough to have books in my house as a child, the hard work of learning to read was done at breakfast with the backs of cereal packets and the labels on sauce bottles (HP even taught me the rudiments of French), allowing me to move on to the more elevated world of tea cards.

Strategies to improve literacy standards in Deaf students – writing

The more astute reader will have observed that I have so far only mentioned reading, not writing. In virtually every case I have observed, both interest and improvement in writing have followed progress in reading rather than preceding or accompanying it. Any literacy improvement plan should be firmly grounded in the promotion and improvement of reading.

Nevertheless, it is never too soon to promote writing skills by trying to raise the profile of writing among students and give it some kudos, for example, concrete rewards as well as commendations in assemblies for good pieces of writing. Modern Teachers of the Deaf (ToDs) should regard themselves as fortunate to be living in the age they do, where the editing and presentation capabilities of Information Communication Technology (ICT) are a significant incentive to try writing. Moreover, with texting, tweeting, blogging and social networking all rampant, it is unlikely that there has ever been a time when it has been so easy to convince Deaf students of the value of text-based methods of communication, if you take a progressive approach. And although present manifestations of the grammar check are of little use to anyone, Deaf or hearing, with language difficulties, nevertheless spell checking (with full training as to the deficiencies of the system on a range of topics from Americanisms to homophones) and the use of the computer's dictionary and thesaurus can be a considerable help, when correctly used.

Every lesson a language lesson

When you have done all this, you can sit back and relax.

Well, actually you can't. Reading English, even when enjoyed, is not necessarily an automatic route to literacy – and certainly it is not the quickest route. All those working with the Deaf, including those who are not directly involved in teaching English, must make the shibboleth 'Every lesson is a language lesson' not merely a reality, but a useful reality. It is easy to sit back and be 'hearing' teachers but waving arms around and using slightly easier words. But that is not what teaching the Deaf is about. Because English is a foreign language for many Deaf students, it requires those working with them to give constant extra support and extra opportunities to use it. This is the hardest part, because it is the least natural to people who have acquired language naturally. It requires constant analysis of how the students are using language, if they are to improve. It is easy to be satisfied because the child has shown understanding of the scientific, mathematical or artistic point that you are trying to get across and not worry about how they express it. Text-based communication is not necessarily the same as English – or at least is not necessarily the same as good English, whether your definition of good English is that it is of General Certificate of Secondary Education (GCSE) standard, or simply that it is clear, unambiguous and comprehensible. So the teaching of the need for clarity in communication should be an essential part of the training of all those working with the Deaf.

But the health warning that comes with these suggestions is that there is no quick fix. Nor should you forget that Deaf students have very different individual needs, and nothing that is done on a whole-school basis will obviate the need for carefully tailored Individual Education Plans.

Points to consider:

- To what extent is English a Modern Foreign Language to Deaf students?
- Are there respects in which this analogy breaks down?

- Is what we know about effective teaching of MFL transferable to teaching the Deaf?
- Are we clear in distinguishing between Language and English/literacy?
- Is it possible to find commercial texts which not only accommodate Deaf students' language delay but also are relevant to their chronological age and their Deaf culture? Or do they need to be produced 'in house'?

2

Communication

Total Communication

When I began teaching the Deaf, the words most commonly used to describe what we did were Total Communication (TC). On the one hand, it was a kind of shorthand to mean that we signed, when many schools still did not. On the other hand, it did have a meaning, which has been lost over the years. We proclaimed no less than that for each student we would use the most suitable combination of elements from speech, aided hearing, lip-reading, writing/reading, sign, finger spelling, drawing, mime and gesture.

The term seems rarely used today. Perhaps those who work with the Deaf are less defensive – or rather, less liable to attack – for using sign than we were then, so they use the word 'signing' more openly. Also, the introduction of teaching in pure BSL in some areas challenged the underlying assumption that whether one put in signs or not, the predominant language mode was likely to be English. But it seems to me that the overall commitment made by using that term is just as relevant today. Unfortunately, it remains just as difficult. TC is very easy from a negative or defensive perspective – TCers don't exclude anything. But in positive terms what do they actually do?

Most of those who work with the Deaf have met students for whom well-structured BSL is no more relevant than speech: they are functioning at a level where mime and gesture, perhaps accompanied by the odd signed word, is likely to be the basis of communication for some time to come. If someone is working alone with that student, or if there is another with them, that is, in the same situation, there is no problem. But what can be done when there is someone else with them who requires much more? And the same problem emerges higher up the communication ladder. What can be done when one is faced with two students, one of whom prefers/needs BSL structure while the other requires speech? If you can speak in English word order while signing in BSL order – congratulations; you are the most total communicator I have ever met.

Fitting communication to individual needs

Some of this is of course the argument of the devil's advocate. Real schools don't just throw students with different communication needs together into random groups. But unless the school can fund one member of staff to every student, or the year groups happen to fall into wonderfully well-matched groups of two or three, this situation will certainly arise. Equally certainly, it will arise in social mixes, or when assemblies or talks by outside speakers need to be interpreted.

It is tempting to waffle, to simply point out the need to look at every single situation on its own merits. Ultimately, that may truly be the only answer that can be given. But before simply taking refuge in that answer it is necessary to look at how it might be possible to resolve the problem and how it is possible to organize the elements. If there is a mixture of modes required at the same time, which should you actually concentrate on – the lowest common denominator, the highest, or should you aim somewhere in the middle?

Using the simplest mode for everyone may sound like the surest way of getting the brightest students bored. But there may be circumstances when it is vital to ensure that everyone gets the information as quickly as possible. To take the most extreme example: should there be a fire, the message that they should proceed in an orderly fashion to the playing field could reasonably be conveyed to everyone with a little mime and pointing quickly enough to avoid its having to be changed to 'Run like hell!'.

Using the highest mode sounds educationally justifiable. It exposes everyone to a mode that will try to raise the standards for the lower ones. But the price of not monitoring carefully what is happening can be total incomprehension at the bottom.

Using an intermediate mode sounds the most downright British way. If faced with an assembly containing all ages from 11–18 no one can be expected to pitch it correctly for all the Deaf. Actually, neither can the person taking the assembly hope to pitch it correctly for all the hearing.

All this may seem reasonable until one takes a step further back and asks to what extent it is possible to satisfactorily define our terms. Signing may be higher than mime, writing higher than drawing, but it is approaching arrogance to think it possible to categorically say which is the higher mode when choosing between speech and sign, or between BSL and English.

What can be learnt from all this? Mostly, as stated at the beginning, the need to establish ground rules for individualized learning in a complex situation; also that the best aid is constant monitoring of what students are understanding, whether by direct questioning or simply by watching their faces for signs of (in)comprehension; and finally, the need to distinguish between formal lessons and informal and social communication. In the formal lessons it should be possible to have handy a variety of resources to support what is intended to be taught. Outside lessons is more of a challenge.

This seems a rather labyrinthine journey to have travelled just to answer the question: Is TC still alive and relevant? But I hope it has raised some questions about the individualization of teaching/learning that are relevant to all those working with Deaf students, whether or not you are of the TC generation.

Teaching vocabulary to Deaf students

The first time I was required to interpret for a Deaf student in a mainstream class was a GCSE Geography lesson on deforestation in the Amazon. In the space between us, I built up a huge forest with a clearing at the centre of the desk, a path threading its way through between the student's pencils to a mighty river in the vicinity of the textbook, running away to the great city which lay beyond the next desk. The massive trees at the edge of the clearing began to fall. The clearing expanded, as the trees were dragged off down the path on their way to the river. It was a veritable triumph of placement and 3D signing. I finally sat back exhausted. The child began to speak. What could she possibly have to say but 'Thank you Mr Brinkley for bringing to life the world of South American logging with such clarity'? Well, actually what she said was 'Mr Brinkley, why you sign so big?'

What it taught me was that signing for students doing academic courses is not a simple matter. When people start out working with the Deaf they tend to think they are interpreters. In fact, what the students want from them is often very different. They want simple summaries of complex points. But even more, they want a guide through the vast technical vocabulary of each subject.

What constitutes technical vocabulary? 'Evaporation' and 'acceleration' look like two equally technical words. To create a sign for evaporation is likely to involve an indication by waggling fingers of steam emerging, possibly from off an E finger, or the kind of finger rubbing that might indicate drying up and disappearing. We teach them the sign and the word. Acceleration, on the other hand, exists in most students' everyday sign vocabulary, not as 'accelerate' but as 'go faster'. Should it be signed as 'go faster' with either an initial 'a' or simply lip pattern to show that we have gone into something more complex than the 'go faster' they first met when Noddy was souping up his taxi?

The signing of technical vocabulary is a major problem for signers. The options are as follows:

1. Finger spell the whole word. This, especially when there are a large number of scientific/technical words that are each several metres long, appears to be a nightmare solution. My inclination is to take refuge in my firm belief that the Deaf find reading back finger spelling at least as difficult as the hearing do and the production of it even more so. There certainly exists a theory which says that in finger spelling the general shape is what matters, rather than getting precisely the right letters. However, this idea is based on the use of finger spelling by the Deaf in normal conversation. Finger spelt words will be few, reasonably well known, rarely technical – and they will not be expecting a test on how to spell them next Friday morning! Even when someone is finger spelling the words clearly and smoothly (and they probably won't, especially if they are not themselves too sure how to spell them) it is still asking a lot to expect students who may never have met the words before to easily see a difference in shape between 'respiration' and 'reproduction', which are not two functions one would want them to confuse.

2. Giving good lip pattern, initialize the word, probably having finger spelt it in full on the first occasion. This is the easy way out. I once heard a parent encouraging a student who was about to do something which no one else at the school had done before, and telling him over and over again that he was to be an ambassador for the Deaf. After she had said this several times, it filtered into my consciousness that I had

no idea what the sign for ambassador might be, so I sneaked a peek. Every time she used the word, she simply finger spelt 'a' and gave lip pattern. But what struck me forcibly was the look of total incomprehension on the child's face. It taught me that the old trick of just initializing is only any use if you have really worked hard on establishing meaning first. Besides, taking into consideration the size of the technical vocabulary used, even in a single subject, there are too many with the same initial for this practice to be anything but confusing.

3. Make up a sign that helps the student to remember the word but does not directly convey the meaning. These can often start as jokes but then become established in the student's mind. One very intelligent girl entered her A-level Maths course still signing algebra as an initial 'a' followed by the sign for brassière. Another student always signed the rows in a spreadsheet as though he were Steve Redgrave. But they are rare – and need to be, if we are to respect the general integrity of signing. These kinds of visual jokes work well in the bestowal of sign names but are not the basis for technical vocabulary.

4. Make up a sign that conveys the word's meaning. This is always likely to be the best solution educationally, but you have to consider the integrity of your signing in public examinations. In some examinations, the Board may specify words that may not be signed. Unfair as this can sometimes seem, it is not a moral problem – just don't sign those words. But if the signing of a word is not banned, how should you approach it? If a sign is highly iconic, is it legitimate to be using it in an exam where hearing students may have only the written form to guide them? Personally, I would not be willing to sign iconically a technical term which I had not used regularly and so expect the student to be familiar with. But if over the period of their course I have given them a lot

of signed vocabulary to learn and they have done so, of course they should reap the reward for learning it.

This final point raises a further problem: in an examination, the person signing may not be one who has taught that student in that particular subject. It is therefore necessary to have some kind of system in place for agreeing and transmitting technical vocabulary between ToDs who share the teaching of the same or related subjects through the school.

Problems of interpreting

A Teacher of the Deaf is not the same as an interpreter. Interpreters have a responsibility to convey to the Deaf person literally every word that is said, and add to that coughs and hiccoughs too. No matter how lost the speaker gets in what they are totally failing to explain, the interpreter will follow them, leading the Deaf person down the convoluted road to nowhere. This is not a criticism of interpreters; that is precisely what the terms of their job require them to do.

However, that is not the job of a ToD, nor of an LSA working with Deaf students. Their job is to take the essence of what is being said and to explain it to students in a language that is comprehensible to them. That in itself is a difficult task. But it also raises the question of what they should do when faced by teachers who waffle. It matters, and not just because delivering everything they say is pointless. It may be possible to argue that since they are trying to build the students' experience of language, anything they expose them to is a good thing. But this fails to take into account the fact that reading sign language is a tiring process.

When I first got a job at a school for the Deaf I was shown round by the deputy head who pointed out to me a particular student with the words, 'If you want to offer him an ice-cream, make sure you start the sentence "Ice-cream – you want one?"' 'Ah!' I replied knowingly. 'So he insists on pure BSL grammatical structure?' She looked at me as if I were a complete idiot, and said 'No. It's just that if the first two words you say don't interest him he stops watching.'

(Incidentally, the same student had a similar attitude to written communication. A friend of his once drew a humorous but insulting cartoon on the board and wrote under it the name of one of the teachers. The aforementioned student punched him in the face. He was not defending the honour of his favourite teacher. The teacher's name began with the same first three letters as his own, so he thought it was himself being insulted.)

The reason why sign reading is exhausting is that it is a full time job. As hearing people, when someone rabbits on repetitiously, or gets off the point, our minds can relax. We know we do not need to take the next bit in. There will be plenty of clues in the tone of the voice, in the pausing, in the change of vocabulary of which we will be semi-aware, to alert us to the fact that our sheep have been returned to, and we need to listen again. The person watching an interpreter very rarely gets comparable clues. They have the choice to watch or not watch; but there is no watching with one eye, as the equivalent of listening with one ear.

Supporting an individual Deaf student

So what is to be done when a teacher goes off on his or her own journey, and it is clear from past experience that it is likely to be a long and uninformative trip?

The options are:

1. Sign and make the Deaf students watch you. This may make you feel morally very good, but if, when the teacher finally gets back to the point, the students are thoroughly confused and no longer concentrating on what they really need to know, not only will you feel less smug, but you will also know that at some point in the near future you will end up having to help them catch up on what they have failed to take in.

2. Sign and make it clear that they do not have to watch unless they want to. If you happen to have got yourself into a conspicuous position where the teacher will notice immediately that you are not signing what they say you may be forced to do this in the interests of international relations. Actually, it always pays to establish with any practitioner with whom you work that there will be times when you don't appear to be signing what they are saying. This does not just apply to when they are drivelling. Often you will find a concept coming up that the students have no idea about and you need to go back and explain it to them from first principles before you can return to what is actually being said.

3. Go over some other aspect of the lesson you think they may not have fully taken in. Given what I have said above about the need to catch up and fill in gaps, this looks like the perfect solution, and often it is. But beware of starting on too big a topic. If you suddenly need to return to your day job and start translating again, you do not want to leave a group that are confused by having missed half the explanation, and being propelled halfway through into something barely connected. Nor do you want to be doing two jobs at once – finishing your previous explanation while listening to what is now being said, knowing you will shortly have to whiz through it. One must admit, however, that the latter is

something that in this profession you will often end up having to do, which is why an in-depth knowledge of the subject is important; without it, it is almost impossible to catch up without asking the teacher to stop. This is not wholly unthinkable, and if you really cannot understand or catch up with what is being said, in fairness to the students that is what you have to do. But it is neither desirable nor remotely comfortable.

4. Chat – I suppose this is the one that would fill most teachers, specialist ToD or mainstream, with horror. Yet it covers three bases – it is relaxing, it develops language, and it is easy to drop quickly if you find the teacher is suddenly back on track.

Points to consider:

- How do students react to mixed modes of communication?
- Do they take in the communication as a whole, or do they each concentrate on the element which represents their own preferred mode?
- When communicating with someone, do they accommodate to that person's preferred mode or persist with their own?
- Is all exposure to signing useful in Deaf children's development? Or is it more useful when it is concentrated?
- Are students exposed to a wide enough range of sign vocabulary? Or is their vocabulary 'localized' to their school/area?

3

Teaching Strategies

Chapter Outline

Differentiation

I don't know whether in the last days of his Premiership Tony Blair made another speech in Sedgefield, pledging that Labour's three priorities were 'Differentiation, differentiation and differentiation', but that seems to have been the focus for every subsequent educational review, Office for Standards in Education (OFSTED) inspection and teacher appraisal. If any teacher has not found that in their school, they are either very lucky, or they have not noticed the alternative spelling of differentiation: w-o-r-k-s-h-e-e t. Teachers who ask how they should be differentiating for the Deaf tend to be of two kinds – the minority who want a deep analysis of the problem, and the majority who want to know if Deaf students can understand the easy worksheet, or will they have to produce another, very easy, one. The most important thing to teach them is that differentiation for the Deaf comes in a number of formats.

> *Differentiation by mode of communication* – although they rarely identify it as differentiation, this is the one that everyone outside our profession immediately thinks of. The train of thought runs in this direction: this student is Deaf; therefore, he/she has a signer; therefore, he/she is no longer a problem. They see the signer, in isolation, as the mode of communication. This is not the case. A teacher standing, facing a class and speaking clearly to them, while a signer also signs to them, is a mode of communication. A teacher standing, back to the class, continuing to say new information while writing on a board notes they have been told to copy, is a different, somewhat inferior, mode of communication. If by the end of the lesson the teacher has avoided the latter, they have demonstrated differentiation just as effectively as by different worksheets.

Differentiation by technological devices – the most obvious are hearing aids, radio aids, cochlear implants and Sound-fields. The maintenance of these devices, as well as ensuring that the students bring the appropriate equipment to lessons, may be our responsibility. But the mainstream teacher has the responsibility to use their end of the equipment properly, to understand what the different devices are, and when they should be used, and when not. Also they, with the coopera-tion of their heads of department, should be responsible for ensuring any DVDs purchased for use with classes have subti-tles, and any equipment used to screen them is capable of connecting to the Radio Telemetry (R/T) system.

Differentiation by curriculum – one of the most hotly con-tested issues in many schools is whether the Deaf should be withdrawn from certain areas of the curriculum. There are two quite distinct considerations.

First, is the nature of the lesson such that it is not appropri-ate for the level of deafness of a particular student? A foreign language that is taught primarily through speaking will be inappropriate for a student who can neither hear the sounds nor articulate them comprehensibly. Music, likewise, will be inappropriate if the student is unable to hear the music well enough to appreciate it. I could have said 'unable to hear the music well enough to complete the required exercises' but I think this would be insulting to the subject. If Music is not about the appreciation of the art form but merely the differ-ence between crotchets and quavers, punctuated by Brahms' principal dates, it is inappropriate for all students, not just the Deaf. Of course, there are areas of music that the Deaf can be involved in (I return to my student with his bagpipe music); I have seen very clever and exciting lessons involving percus-sion put on to ensure the Deaf were included. But to do only this would limit and distort the subject for the others; the same would be true of French if it were decided to ignore spoken French and only do written work so that it was inclusive of the Deaf.

Secondly, are their overall educational needs being met by what they are doing?

There are three areas in which Deaf students need extra input. First, because of their language deprivation they need extra time studying basic literacy. Secondly, because of the gaps in their general knowledge and vocabulary, which like their language deprivation derives from their lack of serendipitous assimilation of information, they need extra 'tutorial' time in most or all of their academic subjects. Finally, they need instruction in a range of areas that are specific to the Deaf: use and upkeep of hearing aids, effective communication with the hearing, legislation and facilities aimed at helping the Deaf, and understanding of deafness; also, depending on their background, some may require signing lessons. And that is to look only at essentials; there remain other areas of Deaf History and Culture which they should rightfully expect to be taught, and which will most likely not happen in mainstream classes. In a day of finite length, this can only be achieved by removing them from less relevant lessons.

Differentiation by grouping – in a sense, this follows on from the above.

On the one hand, it raises the question of when, temporarily or permanently, it is better to remove Deaf students from a mainstream group and for a ToD to teach them discretely. A Science module on sound may seem like an obvious candidate for withdrawal, but much depends on the abilities of the students and the way in which the teacher intends to deliver it: often a Religious Education module on Righteousness or a Maths module on something for which they have no background experience may be a better candidate.

On the other hand, there is the problem of which is the correct group to integrate them into – one with students who have a similar ability in that subject, or one with students who have a similar language ability. In an ideal world this would be an interesting theoretical question, but in reality the behaviour of students in the latter group will often require the former. Often overriding even that is the question of which teacher will be taking the group, and what is their known track record of working with the Deaf?

Differentiation by cultural context – the worst examples of this are those teachers who, presumably to try to show their credentials in Cool, use pop music as their staple example for everything. Databases – let's make one to record our pop CD collection and put in details of 30 albums. Studying a poem – let's rewrite it as a rap, or a pop song in the style of . . . . But there are plenty of other examples of soaps or radio personalities or famous hearing people that are just as meaningless to many Deaf students. When expressed in these terms it is not the most difficult one for teachers to understand, but it is probably the one which, left to their own devices, they are most likely to miss. The moral is, don't leave them to their own devices! Keep a close eye on work that is coming up.

Differentiation by acoustic/visual conditions – if you work in an old school you will be told there is nothing that can be done about this; if you work in a new school you will be told it was all sorted when the place was built. Neither is likely to be fully true.

When showing the class a video or PowerPoint, don't turn off the light making the room so dark that the Deaf student cannot see the signer. I once took a group of Deaf students on a tour (prearranged, and they knew we were bringing Deaf) of a power station where a recorded voice announced in total pitch dark the details of what they were going to see next, until suddenly the exhibit was lit up for a moment. I used to know a Deaf woman so notorious for chatting that when she went out at night she took a pair of brilliant white gloves with her so people could 'hear' her in the dark. But I would have needed fluorescent ones in this case.

Teachers who throw windows open onto a road rumbling with heavy traffic to let some fresh air in, may be failing to differentiate the environmental needs of Deaf students. Likewise with those who stick notices over the holes on the echo-deadening soundboards.

Also under this heading will come optimum seating position for lip-reading, if required. And if being at the front is not required, why do the Deaf still so often get placed there?

Differentiation by support – this means not only the person in support (LSA, CSW [Communication Support Worker] or ToD), but also their function. They may be there to sign, to lip-speak, to act as note taker, to help with completing the work or any combination thereof. Also, their time allotment becomes a point of differentiation. Some Deaf students will require a full-time presence, others an interpreter just for the introduction to the lesson and yet others just an occasional drop-in to sort out any problems that may have arisen.

Differentiation by language level – verbally this is not a problem. If a teacher is using language that is over the heads of the students, unless it is so inappropriate that it is over the head of the support worker as well, they will naturally remould it as they sign it into something comprehensible. Usually, the problem lies with written text, whether notes on the blackboard, textbooks, examination papers – or worksheets!

Differentiation by presentation – if you entirely sort out the language problem, this probably won't be needed, but, in the expectation that the Language Solution Day is still somewhere on the horizon, clear presentation can help clarify several things that the language obscures. Support workers will usually only get a preview of these things when staff are preparing exam papers, but the same principles apply just as much to a range of things from PowerPoints to worksheets.

- Relevant and clear illustrations, preferably labelled, are useful; pretty illustrations put in to fill up some white space are simply confusing.
- Important words should be emphasized. Preferably, use bold or underline rather than italic. Many Deaf students don't really associate italic with emphasis, perhaps because they don't have the experience of hearing the emphasis that someone puts on words that are italicized in a book. But don't overdo the emphasis to the point where you have more words emphasized than not.
- Never link questions or steps in a sequence into a single sentence with 'and'. Set each out on a separate line. That way there is a chance that both will be answered/done.
- If you are giving a selection of answers with which to fill in blanks, put the answers before the text, where they will be seen, not after it.

Someone, I don't know whether it was Qualifications and Curriculum Authority (QCA) or the United Nations, has apparently declared it a great idea to start an examination paper with a prolonged and almost wholly irrelevant fairy story called a context. This is hard for Deaf students to read, and confuses them into thinking there may be useful information in it – so they try to incorporate it into their answers which then become wrong. Unfortunately, the regulations for signing public examinations forbid us to say, 'Just skip that rubbish and get on with the questions.' But if you know teachers who habitually put this kind of thing into their school texts, try to discourage them.

The importance of humour

If you ask yourself the question, 'What do Deaf students most miss out on in speech as a result of their deafness?', depending on your personal proclivities, you may be tempted to answer either important information or word endings. In my opinion, the answer is neither of those. It is humour.

If you think of the very term schoolboy (or schoolgirl) humour, what comes immediately to mind are terrible puns and knock-knock jokes: in other words – the untranslatable. I remember the very first tutor group that I had when I began teaching the Deaf. One of them went to hospital for a minor operation (in those days doctors still did operations in preference to 'procedures') and I agreed to buy a Get Well card for the class to sign. 'And make sure', were their final words to me, 'that it's funny!' It was the hardest task I've ever been given. There were a thousand humorous cards, but every single one was based on a pun the patient would not understand, from one showing a Shelley-like figure ('I was going to write you a poem but I didn't want to make you verse') to a patient stroking a kid goat ('You'll soon be feeling a little butter'). In the end I just went for the one with the funniest picture, a bunny surgeon, and ignored the reference to a hoperation; as Homer Simpson would say, 'It's funny because the doctor's a rabbit!'

That was the first time I realized what a massive part of life they were excluded from. Of course it is possible to explain a pun. Sometimes if a teacher makes that kind of joke and a student asks why people are laughing, you may need to do so. But whatever the length of your explanation, it will be short of humour. It's often better to just roll your eyes and say, 'Hearing joke'.

What about Deaf humour? Much adult Deaf humour is based on the discomfiture, or possibly slow lingering deaths, of interpreters, or on other adult situations. Alternatively, it can be based on very subtle variations of the grammar or formation of BSL signs, one sign morphing into another, or one hand which has had a role in a two-handed sign suddenly being withdrawn to a new function leaving the other hand in a desperate plight. However, for children who are really only learning the language, often in a context of SSE rather than BSL, it must be rather like a lecturer I once had who used to tell jokes in English but deliver the punch line in German.

More realistically, for Deaf children, humour is likely to be slapstick. And in that too they are often deprived. As a hearing child in Primary School, our end-of-term treat would, as often as not, be that our Head would hire a set of shorts by Charlie Chaplin or Laurel and Hardy to show on the school's ancient and silent projector. Much the same diet was available on children's television: genuine silents such as Buster Keaton, more modern efforts from Laurel and Hardy, in which they spoke, but the speech was wholly irrelevant, and live custard pie fights from the likes of Mr Pastry. It was the staple comedy diet of hearing and Deaf alike. Even adult audiences had the likes of Norman Wisdom. He was made a national hero in Albania. He probably was in Deafland too, and for the same reason: no language was required to understand the humour.

But this confluence in the media of the humorous interests of both Deaf and hearing is rare now. I still remember how excited the Deaf were when Mr Bean was at his height, and 'their' humour was for a short time universally trendy.

Other forms of humour can come and go. There was once a trend for Deaf students to make a statement which seemed possible, wait for you to believe it, and then deny its authenticity by making the sign for 'joke' (very similar to the film *Bill and Ted's Excellent Adventure* where people make statements, and

then tag the word 'not' onto the end of the sentence). It is difficult to convey just how funny this is when it has been done for
the twenty-third time that day! It is possible to discourage it
temporarily by promising the students something really nice,
and then signing 'joke' after it, but it does not make you popular.
And beware, it will come round again.

This has been a lengthy diagnosis of the problem. Inevitably,
the prescription to cure it is not a simple one. But I firmly
believe that it is necessary to make some effort to introduce a
little humour to compensate for what they are missing.

- Be extravagant physically. Students love this, especially when
  it goes wrong. The high point of my career to some students
  was when I attempted to prove that an empty drink can was
  empty by inverting it over my head. It wasn't empty. You can't
  plan that kind of disaster, but if you take enough risks it will
  happen regularly.
- Use stupid examples. Why ask how many apples you have if
  you start with 37 and give 9 away, when it is no more difficult
  to ask how many dancing hippos you have left if you start
  with 37 and hide 9 in the Geography Room?
- Throw in some sign puns. Even if you cannot bear to point at
  your bottom for Arsenal you can at least try pointing at the
  toe and knee for Tony or finger spelling potooooooooo for
  potatoes (8 'o's – geddit?)
- Have a supply of funny pictures on your computer and throw
  them in from time to time just to enliven your PowerPoints,
  without bothering about relevance. Googling 'Cute Pets' is as
  good a starting point as any.
- When interpreting, introduce an occasional exaggerated
  impression of the person you are signing for. It is a fine line to
  walk. The ones that you can have the most fun in parodying
  are likely to be the ones who like it least.

Also important is to realize that, by and large, Deaf students do not 'get' sarcasm. No matter how confident you are that your entire facial expression, body language and multichannel signing is screaming 'NOT' when you tell a student who has just broken a keyboard, 'That was *really* clever, wasn't it!' everyone else in the room will immediately break theirs as well, in order to show that they are no less clever.

Countering avoidance strategies

This is definitely not the most politically correct section of the book. But it contains some abiding truths.

The first is 'Beware of the Noddy syndrome.' Many Deaf students have learned that when Teacher is rabbiting on, and they have not understood a word, the best way to keep Teacher in a happy mood is to smile and nod their head at periodic intervals.

Let us be honest, this is by no means the prerogative of the Deaf. I recently read *Home With Alice* by Stephen Fallon, an American who went to stay in the Gaeltacht of Ireland to learn Gaelic. He said that the most useful phrase he ever learnt was the approximate equivalent of 'OK!' and whenever a native speaker was regaling him with a story that he found wholly incomprehensible he would introduce this phrase every time the speaker paused for breath, since it encouraged him to go on without asking any embarrassing questions that might show up the listener's incomprehension, and it might eventually lead him into a different area that the listener actually understood.

Let us suppose that you are faced with Noddy syndrome and not simply a charming, happy student who is so engrossed in your lucid explanation, of which they understand every single word that they do not wish to make any comment which might cause you to stop. There are two approaches: the educationalist's and the psychologist's.

The educationalist will stop and ask a question to test the student's comprehension of the last thing they said. If this proves negative they will do the same for the preceding concept; and so backwards until they get to the first thing that the student genuinely understood. This may well turn out to be 'Good morning!'

The psychologist will cut his losses and use the words for which the student has waited so patiently: 'That's it. Finished! Understand? Good. Let's start something else.' You then go over exactly the same ground, but at a lower level. This stops the student worrying about all the stuff they didn't understand, and gives them a clean sheet. And if by any remote chance they actually did understand you the first time, explain to the OFSTED inspector it was reinforcement.

The exact opposite of Noddy syndrome is Pow syndrome. In this the student avows total incomprehension of anything the teacher has said. This is done by passing the straightened forefingers of both hands simultaneously from the front to the back of the head at a height of about 2 inches while spitting out an explosive 'Pow!' Some students, with slightly greater enunciation facility, may substitute the word 'Whoooosh!' This performs the same function as Noddy, that is, it obviates the student's need to think, but is more subtle, because it puts the teacher under pressure instead of the student. It says, 'This is your fault. You are not explaining it in a way I can understand. *And you can't prove otherwise!*' A really determined Power can keep it up for ages, with the obduracy of those small children who ask 'Why?' at the end of every statement you make, no matter how simple. And in both cases it is pointless to try to explain: your explanation will be met with another 'Why?' or another 'Pow!'

I am not of course suggesting that every response of 'Pow!' you ever evoke is an avoidance strategy. Often we all fail to make ourselves clear. But you will soon get to know which students are serial Powers.

There is a story of a driver in Suffolk who stopped and asked a man in a field, 'How do I get to Ipswich from here?' The man thought long and hard before finally replying, 'If I was wanting to get to Ipswich I wouldn't come this way at all', with which wisdom he walked away. On the same principle, the best way of avoiding an intense Powing is not to go down that road in the first place. If a student regularly Pows algebra, get some compasses out and pretend it's going to be geometry until they have accidentally learnt something. Then if the Powing starts, put the responsibility onto the student. Since they claim your signing is incomprehensible, ask them to explain what they know about the generality or the basics or past experience of the subject; thereafter build on their explanation using *their* signs and terminology.

The clicking of middle finger against thumb which designates Finished is, if anything, more irritating than even a Pow. It can occasionally be replaced by the beckoning of the right hand at the level of the right shoulder which signifies Before. Either way, the message is the same: we've done this before and we're blowed if we're doing it again.

The nuances of this can range from the perfectly legitimate, 'You were off yesterday and we did it with the other teacher' to the far more probable 'I think I remember this word from three years ago – and I didn't like it!' The idea of extending work they have already done, by working in greater depth or detail, is not a popular one. Had Shakespeare and Newton been Deaf, it is unlikely we would have *Henry IV Part II* and the Second Law of Motion.

Of course there are times when you and they just have to plunge in and do it, whatever their complaints. But it does pay to anticipate and avoid Finished.

Try to avoid dredging up the same old PowerPoints and pictures that you have used before, even if most of the material on them is new. Try not to use the same main words in the title. If you know you are going to have to continue with something similar or, worse still, repeat the lot because they clearly haven't understood it, make a big thing at the end of lesson about not having quite finished that topic off, and asking them to remind you next time to do the rest.

Strategies for students with language difficulties

Although this book is aimed at those working with the Deaf, I sincerely believe that a good deal of what I have said is relevant to those who teach students who also have language difficulties that are a result of other causes than deafness. I do not think that generally ToDs are given credit for what they could show other members of staff in this area. So in this section I have tried to pull together some observations that I believe apply to students with and without hearing losses in equal measure. Bring these or your own ideas up at subject-based department meetings, and amaze your colleagues.

A combination of The National Curriculum, OFSTED and the Eleventh Plague of Educational Consultants has established that all shall be cursed who do not begin their lesson with a plenary session, preferably with a PowerPoint. There is nothing wrong with that so long as you do not outstay the attention span of your students. A good teacher moves on to a practical exercise as soon as their presentation loses the attention of the students. A very good teacher moves on to a different exercise just before their presentation loses the attention of the students.

My general experience teaches me that the only good PowerPoint is a blank one. Start from nothing or perhaps a single word. Establish what the students know about it. Put in their definition. Add some illustration. Of course, there will be teachers who will say you are just idle, just making it up as you go along; they will contrast their beautifully crafted efforts which took them so long to prepare. But the truth is often that the PowerPoint they (or perhaps someone else in their department) took so long to produce will be used for class after class, year after year. The class will have no ownership of what is in it. Furthermore, the students I am talking about won't understand a quarter of what it says.

Nor is starting from scratch as labour unintensive as it sounds. Not only do you need a very clear idea of what information you are going to be trying to tease out and how to present it, but you will need to have ready all possible illustrations you will require; you only want to be desperately scrabbling around Googling one up when a student produces a really brilliant idea that you could never have anticipated.

Teach the concrete before the abstract though this may make a nonsense of trying to explain lesson objectives at the beginning of the lesson. Most of these children are so far from abstract patterns of thought that they need to see something concrete happen before they know there is something here which requires a name, never mind what that name might be.

Never try to anticipate more than one problem in advance. If your opening spiel becomes a list of things they need to watch out for, they will not only forget the solutions, but half of them will forget what the aim is and end up trying to emulate the mistakes. Set them off with a clear sense of what they are aiming to do, and wait for them to find the problems themselves. Then run round like a fly with an azure fundament answering questions as they turn up. It does not matter if you have to answer the same question several times, because each student will be learning the solution at the only time in their life that they want the solution – namely, at the exact moment they have the problem.

When a student in a high group finds a difficulty, you can assume it will also prove a problem for several others, so it is worthwhile stopping the rest of the class to discuss it. In lower groups the problem that a student finds may well be so bizarre that you will never meet it again. It is better to have to show the same thing to three or four individuals than to confuse everyone but one. The only time it is worth stopping everyone is when it is your fault, as you find you have given them wholly bum information.

When a child gives a wrong answer, it is very tempting to encourage the child by saying, 'Well, you're sort of on the right lines'. Occasionally you may have to, if that is the first time in 3 months they have answered a question, or they look as if they will burst into tears if you tell them they are wrong. But to produce some amazing piece of casuistry to enable you to segue from their wrong answer to your right one is a recipe for disaster. Be very aware that they will not remember your clever explanation. They will remember their wrong answer. And they will remember you told them it was right.

Another common but disastrous scenario is asking a hard question to see if anyone can get it right. Of course, no one does and you will end up having to tell them the answer. With a really bright class this strategy works, not merely because there may be someone who knows the answer, but also because when intelligent students get answers wrong it gives you an insight into how they are thinking. When a student from the bottom classes gets an answer wrong, it is because they are guessing. Even if you say, 'Now stop guessing, and think hard about what we have done before', it will make no difference. They will still guess ever more wildly.

Demonstrations work better than explanations – but only if you do them correctly. If you make a mistake don't try to waffle your way over it, or lose them in a blinding flurry of key clicking. Admit you've got it wrong. Repeat that several times as you go back to the beginning. Then show them the whole thing again correctly. Twice if necessary.

Go into many lessons and at some point the students will end up copying notes from the board. If you ask staff to justify this exercise, they are unlikely to give the reply, 'It gives me and them a rest!' though that is probably the most honest, and possibly the most educationally justifiable, reply. You are more likely to be told that it gives them essential revision notes. Forty years ago this was a reasonable answer. In the very first school in which I worked, the only way of reproducing notes for students was a jelly mould. (I am not making this up. You wrote the notes in mirror writing using special ink on top of a tray of special jelly. The jelly was heated slightly, and pieces of paper pressed to the top took up an impression from the ink.) But in an age of computer printers and photocopiers I seriously doubt whether this note-taking exercise is worth the candle, compared with periodically giving them a nicely printed, and correct, summary sheet. Others, however, will say that the act of writing it down will help imprint it in their memories. This is definitely not the case for students with poor language skills. For this to work, a student needs to read at the very least a full phrase, preferably a sentence, hold it in their memory, and then write it on the page. Students with poor language skills at best transfer a word at a time, more often two or three letters. This is why not only do they not remember what they have written, but also if they ever do try to revise from it, it will be unreadable because they will have missed out big chunks as they skipped from the pair of letters they were copying to the next occurrence of the same pair of letters a line or so down. You can reassure them that this is called haplography, and mediaeval monks did it all the time when copying books in Latin which they didn't really understand.

I have mentioned clear sequencing in the section on differentiation, but I think it is worth repeating. The Third Law of Sequencing says that even if, perhaps especially if, the steps you want them to follow are set out in writing as a reminder for them, do not use too many steps in the same exercise. The dreaded haplography will appear and they will end up with two steps missing from the middle of the sequence. The Second Law of Sequencing says you should never link two steps in the same sentence with 'and'. Some will do the first part. Some will do the second part. But absolutely no one will do them both. I had once supposed that the First Law of Sequencing was so well known to everyone that there was no point in teaching it – but over the years I have seen the law broken so often, even in public exams supposedly written by experts, that I will state it. Never test the subtleties of sequencing on a student if you actually want them to get it right. The correct sequence in the instruction 'Before lighting the touch-paper, ensure you have put on your safety gear' may seem entirely clear to you. It will also seem entirely clear to the student. . . .

Points to consider:

- Given the amount of differentiation that many Deaf students require, is it reasonable to expect every mainstream teacher to be able to accommodate a Deaf student in their class?
- Or should there be an unofficial 'driving test', so that only those teachers who show ability/aptitude in this area continue to do so?
- What level of extra support (human/resource/financial/ class size) is required to enable a teacher to give adequate differentiation to Deaf students?
- How much overlap is there between the skills required to work with the Deaf, and those required to work with hearing students with language disorders or other learning difficulties?
- Is there a danger that by conflating these two areas we associate Deaf students too much with disorders rather than with simply having a different first language?
- What can we learn from (and contribute to) those staff working with students who have English as a second language?

4

Emotional and Psychological Issues

Chapter Outline

Differences between Deaf and hearing students

The frequently heard phrase 'Deaf way different!' tends to make the ToD's hackles rise. Too often it is an arrogance meaning little more than 'I can't be bothered to learn how to do it your way, even though my way is less efficient, and sometimes downright wrong.'

This is however not always true. I remember a student who had a completely original way of calculating accurately and at lightning pace, by wiggling his fingers at a blur in a peculiar way which no one else was ever able to understand, nor he to properly explain.

It is also indisputable that there are certain tendencies of the Deaf cultural milieu that they take as natural, but by which the hearing are driven to distraction – though I am perhaps here only speaking on behalf of the middle class tendency, rather than the hearing generally. There is, for example, the total disregard for beginning on time; the indisposition towards hurrying anything; the lack of tact in making personal remarks ('New dress? It's horrible: makes you look fat.') This kind of thing does raise the question of what is acceptable and what should be taught. Since much of their time is likely to be spent in a hearing environment, should they not at least be shown what the hearing way is in these situations? Or is this a kind of cultural imperialism which just takes us back to the days when the Deaf regarded the Royal National Institute for the Deaf (RNID) as Really Not Interested in the Deaf?

But whatever you decide to do in these instances, there is no excuse for interfering with Deaf culture just because it is different. I remember a profoundly deaf student who when Walkmen first arrived came to school with one and spent much of his break time listening to it. Fascinated by what kind of music would be appealing to someone with so little hearing I asked if I could listen. It was bagpipe music. I suppose I could have tried to persuade him that there were other forms of music he could listen to, but I would have been wasting my time. This was something he could sense. Nothing I could say to him would make him able to appreciate Vaughan Williams.

The Deaf way is different, and that is what those who work with the Deaf not only have to understand, but also get across to other staff.

Problems of mainstreaming

Were I to have been writing this book at the beginning of my career instead of at its end, it would have been written as a guide to working in a school for the Deaf, with this section dedicated to helpful comments for others who were working in units attached to mainstream schools, or within mainstream classes. Although happily some schools for the Deaf continue to survive, mainstreaming has become the dominant philosophy.

It is not my intention to make this chapter a sour grousing at the way things have changed, nor a call to the barricades to fight for the return of special schools. But before the generation who worked in them go off to join the generation who fought in the trenches, I think it behoves me to make an analysis of what was lost when those schools were closed, because only then will it be seen clearly what the mainstream schools need to do to satisfy the emotional and psychological, as well as the educational, needs of their Deaf students.

The biggest difference lies in communication of information. Whatever effort a school may put into record keeping, however many coordination meetings may be organized, the results will be as nothing compared with having a situation where every member of staff you meet from daybreak till sundown is interested in exactly the same students as you, and therefore is not only willing, but eager, to hear your moans, worries or incredible breakthrough in Deaf pedagogy.

In spite of the fact that we are told that we are living in the midst of a revolution in communications, too often in mainstream schools the solution to all communications is still held to be meetings and more meetings. Our meetings generally took place because they were necessary in that decisions had to be made that could not just be straw polled in everyday conversation. But they were mercifully short because we did not need to have an agenda full of things that had already been discussed more casually.

Although the charge by the Deaf that closing schools for the Deaf would kill sign language proved wrong in the case of those areas where the bulk of Deaf students were kept together in a single school, employed as a kind of centre of excellence for Deaf education, it is hard to judge the effect where Deaf students were much more thinly spread. And there was a much more subtle way in which the quality of Deaf students' signing experience declined when they were mainstreamed.

Special schools provided, or at least had the potential to provide, a total signing environment. There are two aspects to such an environment. The first is social. It gives the child the confidence that wherever they are in school they are surrounded by people who can communicate with them. The second aspect is educational: that at all times they should be surrounded not just by people who *can* sign, but who *do* sign. So the student begins, albeit belatedly, to get that experience of building up language not just from what they are taught, but also from what they see around them. I suspect that if all of us who were there were asked to clap our hands on our heart and say that we always did so, the noise of palms hitting chests would not be thunderous. And of course whenever we took them out to integrate into mainstream, the spell was again broken. But the potential was there.

In mainstream, this is never achieved. The Deaf, even where there is a substantial Deaf presence, are always outnumbered by 1,000 to 30. Even if you declare one day a year to be Deaf Awareness Day only a few dedicated and confident signers will go around signing other than when absolutely required to do so.

The best that can really be done in mainstream is to promote Deaf Awareness. This works up to a point. You can offer basic signing lessons to every hearing person, child and adult, in the building; you can even enforce them. You can put more advanced Sign Language as an option onto the hearing curriculum. You can lecture all staff termly on communication, differentiation and Deafication. But you do not achieve Deaf Awareness; or perhaps it would be fairer to say that you may achieve Deaf Awareness but you do not achieve Deaf Understanding. Only by working directly with, as opposed to in the same building as, the Deaf, do you build the understanding of their problems that you need to inform your management, be it classroom management or management of the whole school.

In schools for the Deaf, the whole management structure from top to bottom was not only Deaf aware, but also positively aimed at the Deaf. Consequently, when something unusual was arranged one did not continually need to worry whether interpreters had been organized, or if the language levels of new textbooks had been checked for suitability.

There were no deaf-unfriendly assemblies containing singing, knock-knock jokes, references to pop culture or simply contemporary news items, improvised sketches involving simultaneous talking by several people; no unsignables such as non-sense rhymes or list of books of the Bible. (I signed Numbers and Acts. I could probably have signed Revelations more spectacularly than I did, but by then I had lost the will to live.)

The accusation often made against us was that we developed a ghetto mentality, and lost touch with standards in mainstream schools, with the result that we did not have high enough expectations of Deaf students. There may have been schools where either by choice or by geographical necessity this was true. But in most it was not. Integration into local mainstream schools for many lessons was the reality.

On the one hand, there was a social integration: most went for PE/Games. Two-a-side rugby is an uninspiring game for a year group in a small school – particularly when someone is absent. Most went for lower school Art and Cookery, until the latter became Theoretical Nutrition Studies and the scones disappeared under a pile of worksheets. On the other hand, there was a more academic integration, with students joining mainstream classes for lessons up to GCSE, for whatever subjects they were best at.

The sheer logistics of getting students to and from lessons in the mainstream school half a mile away were horrendous, and undoubtedly cost time; but while not actually being Time Lords, we were able to manufacture a good deal of time because we had total control over the rest of the curriculum. If we decided it would be a good idea for Y7 and Y8 to have Geography at the same time with the same teacher – behold it was so. It might appear that all being on the same site will make integration so much easier. But it is the all-constraining rigidity of the mainstream timetable that makes it so difficult to provide for Deaf students' individual needs.

The fact that we could write our own timetable gave us the flexibility to put in not just extra 'tutorial' time as backup for their work in specific subjects, but also lessons such as Deaf Studies or Communication Skills, which are very difficult to fit into a mainstream timetable. The more integration there is, the less chance of fitting in material, which would be primary for the Deaf but is only secondary for the hearing.

I am sure that there is much that can be said in favour of mainstreaming in terms of social mix, experience of communication with the hearing, more challenge for the better students and so on. But, not unreasonably, you will never find the same flexibility and accommodation to individual needs in a school of over 1,000 that you will in a school of under 100.

It is absolutely essential that the school is sited within easy access of a mainstream school into which Deaf students can integrate. But it is also important that Deaf students can, if necessary, be put in a protective separate environment. Many Deaf students do not require this but it must be appreciated that among severely or profoundly deaf people some 45 per cent now have additional disabilities. Where these additional problems are predominantly physical, they could largely be overcome by additional support in mainstream; but where they are emotional, behavioural or related to learning ability (or combinations thereof), they are much more difficult to resolve. It is the number and broad nature of these additional disabilities that require provision for the Deaf to become increasingly 'special' in the old sense.

Points to consider:

- Is it possible to distinguish the social and pedagogical aspects of mainstreaming?
- If it is possible, is it desirable? And what would the balance be between the two in evaluating success or failure?
- What really drives the decision on how and where to accommodate Deaf Education? What part is played by parental choice? Financial constraints? Government education policy? Educational theory?
- Will the accommodation of Deaf Education inevitably mirror the accommodation for visual impairment and/ or Moderate Learning Difficulties (MLD) and/or Emotional and Behavioural Difficulties (EBD)?

5

Technology

Technical aids and other equipment

Technology to aid hearing is supposed to be our forte, the thing we are known for outside the profession. One day an elderly lady, otherwise unknown to the school, arrived, complete with dog, at the School for the Deaf and asked for a confidential word with the Head. Unsure whether she was going to offer the school a handsome legacy or complain about our students throwing things over her fence, he went to see her. She pointed at the dog, complained that it was going deaf and asked if he could fix it up with a hearing aid.

This chapter is not going to be a handbook on how to operate and test hearing aids, radio aids and cochlear implants. If I were to write such a chapter I might as well ask my publisher to print it on rice paper so that it can be eaten in a few months' time when changes in technology have made the details wholly anachronistic. Besides, the complexity of the new technology, and the expense that goes with it, has almost entirely changed what we can do.

When I began teaching, if you wanted to test an analogue hearing aid, you could listen through a stetoclip and if you didn't like what you heard you could fiddle with a couple of basic controls and put it in a test box; if you still were not happy, you had a selection of spare aids which you could easily adjust to the right setting for that student, and Robert was your Aunt's husband. Now in the digital age, no Health Authority can afford to be handing out spare hearing aids like sweeties, and even if we had them it requires expensive computerized equipment and a lot of training to set them up. Much the same principle applies to cochlear implants. So the responsibility tends to devolve to the Health Authority.

Even R/T is beginning to go the same way. When I began we had a technician who could fix most problems with a soldering iron and a jeweller's screwdriver. Now even the simplest problem such as a blown fuse seems to end up being sent back to the manufacturer for a major servicing at great cost.

The Soundfield system, if your school is lucky enough to have one, is a two-edged sword, the more so if, as in many cases, it is 'looked after' by a ToD. The problem is that it becomes seen by many staff as 'the Deaf thing' and although your entering the room with a clutch of Deaf students may remind them to use it, it also makes them liable to give up on it when there are no Deaf students in sight. No matter how often they are told that Soundfields are for every student, those who are technophobes or who aver that 'shouting at the little so and sos was good enough for my father, and it's good enough for me' will use a lack of Deaf students as their excuse to leave the microphone hanging on the wall.

For the benefit of anyone who has never encountered a Soundfield system, it is a simple amplification system in which the teacher wears a microphone and broadcasts through speakers placed all around the room. It saves the strain on their voice caused by over projection to the back, to ensure people there have equal access to the teaching process – what we used to call 'shouting over the ones making a noise at the front'. More to the point, it enables those at the back to hear clearly. It is not primarily aimed at the Deaf, though it has the advantage that the teacher's R/T microphone can be plugged into the control box, rather than having to be worn, and that any video clips or similar things that are broadcast will go automatically through the R/T system without cables and wires having to be changed over and plugged into television sets and so on. Nevertheless, it has to be said that since there is no guarantee that the settings, let alone the actual acoustic conditions, of every Soundfield are identical, it is not really viable to balance radio aids accurately to a setting that will work everywhere.

The Soundfield works to overcome the principle that when a teacher is slightly difficult to hear, it gives students who are not 100 per cent committed to education an excuse to switch off. In fact, experiments have taken place in recent years in which students who were poor listeners, but had no hearing loss, were given what effectively were low-powered hearing aids to keep them attentive to the teacher. The consequence is that most complaints of Soundfields not working come from students at the back; half from those who find it really useful and have difficulty without it; half from those who hope that if they complain when it is working perfectly well it might get switched off and stop keeping them awake.

Also it has to be borne in mind that at any given time a room full of students is likely to contain at least one case of temporary conductive deafness about which you, in fact about which the student, may not be aware. I repeat this statistic frequently in an attempt to scare teachers. Since they do not know which student it is, they should cover themselves by using the Soundfield at all times.

Our role is therefore increasingly to test systems. When you find a problem, if you are lucky enough to have your own technician, well and good. Otherwise, fight your Health Authority, or whoever is responsible for replacements, for the quickest possible turn-round. Actually, the quickest possible turn-round that is compatible with them sending the correct object is an even better aim. Within this, try to maintain the best possible relationship with them, especially if you have no long-term written guarantee from them that they will service the school. Having to rely on parents to take children into the hospital to obtain replacements/repairs is the nightmare scenario.

Use of hearing aids

We can look at hearing aid systems until we are blue in the face, but it only puts off the awful day when we have to examine the questions of how efficient they are and how we deal with a situation in which students are unwilling to wear them. If you inhabit one of those schools which seem to appear in audiology books where streams of happy Deaf children love their hearing aids, hate to be parted from them for a moment and never ever leave them switched off in the hope the ToD won't notice – congratulations. Please pass straight on to the next chapter.

Now that the inhabitants of Fairyland have left us, those (few?) of us who remain can have an honest discussion. We all know that there are some students who really value their Behind the Ear aids (BTEs), In the Ear aids (ITEs), cochlear implants or R/T, and who can become quite distressed if the equipment is not working properly, or they are unable to use it for some other reason, such as ear infections. We also know that there are others who, though they do not recognize the fact so consciously, become very noisy, or quiet, or exhibit bizarre behaviours when their equipment is not working.

But especially we know that many of them reject all or some of this equipment, either by outright refusal to wear it or by leaving it switched off, with flat batteries and so on.

There are essentially three lines of argument as to why this happens. The first is that they reject them because of lack of consistency. If only parents would make them wear them at home all the time. If only every teacher would check constantly whether they were switched on. If only Health Authorities would replace broken aids immediately. The problem then arises as to our moral, or indeed our legal, right to force them to wear aids that they have decided they do not want to wear any longer. It is of course possible to stipulate on some kind of school contract that the hearing aids are to be worn as a part of the school uniform on pain of some dire penalty. But can you guarantee that every parent will be willing to sign it, rather than going with it to the European Court of Human Rights or, worse still, the local newspaper?

The second theory is that the problem is essentially one of attitude. They do not wish to be conspicuous. Wearing equipment that hearing students do not use draws attention to their deafness, makes them look different and is altogether uncool. If this were really the reason, I would expect to have observed two phenomena. First, I would expect that the more miniaturized the equipment becomes, the less unpopular it is. I am not old enough to remember the days of body worn aids, and speech trainers the size of a small Suffolk village. But I have seen the equipment get smaller without becoming any more popular. Secondly, I would expect it to be less popular where there are only a few Deaf, not wanting to be conspicuous, and more popular when the Deaf are in strength or, in the case of schools for the Deaf, in the majority. Again I have not noticed this being the case.

If this is all about image, it may be necessary to rethink policy. In my experience, new technology is always rolled out from the bottom. When there is enough money available to supply a single year group with, for example, miniaturized R/T, the decision is 'Start with Year 7 because they are the most consistent users, and gradually build it up through the school.' But if it is an image question, should there not be a real effort made to win over the older students who are the role models?

There is indeed a risk there, given that the older students are the ones most likely to have rejected the older technology. Will their experience of the old technology prejudice them against seeing the improvement in the new, in the same way that I believe some of the adult Deaf are virulently against it because of their bad experiences of yet older technology?

But the third and most heretical theory is that maybe the students are right.

I understand the dangers of applying an analogy from the hearing world to that of the Deaf, when I do not have enough personal knowledge of the latter to be sure the comparison is accurate. However, that is not going to stop me. I once owned a cheap transistor radio, in an area where reception, at least of Radio 4, was not wonderful. The result was a fair amount of crackle and interference. When there was a programme being broadcast which really interested me, the interference did not bother me; in fact, I scarcely noticed it. But when there was a less interesting programme, the crackle annoyed me so much that I would often turn it off.

When, as we frequently do, we 'prove' to students (well, at least to ourselves) that they hear x per cent better with techno-logical equipment, we do so by giving them exercises on which they are required to concentrate. They will concentrate on the exercise. They will perform better with the equipment. We blithely tell them how that proves they need to use it all the time. But they are not concentrating with that degree of intensity all, or even most, of the time.

If this is so, we need to base our policy on a 'need to hear' basis, being much more flexible and much more selective about the situations in which we press for them to wear the equip-ment. To take an example which may well cause apoplexy to the orthodox: in what situation is it most important for a Deaf child to wear a hearing aid? Now that I have been almost deafened myself by your shouts of 'In all School lessons', 'In all lessons where a teacher is talking', 'In all lessons where there is group discussion', may I suggest that the correct answer might actually be 'When crossing the road'! Much as I deprecate the idea of a student missing a single word of wisdom from me, I suspect that their missing it will be less destructive to them than being hit by a truck.

The joke I am most tired of hearing is from the teacher who says 'Why are your hearing aids in your pocket? Are your pockets Deaf? Hahahaha!' Just once I'd like the student to have the courage to reply 'My hearing aids are in my pocket in case I suddenly need them.' Every time we nag that student to put them in their ear when they don't feel they need them, we bring closer the day when they decide to leave them at home to avoid the problem. I need glasses for some things. I call to witness all the people who have had to repeat things they've signed to me, after waiting for me to get close enough! But I would take it very ill if they demanded I wore glasses all the time, so as to suit them and not me.

Our expertise should be to immediately recognize situations where students are starting to experience problems, and suggest they use their aids for a while. Both sides should recognize that it is only a suggestion, though it is an informed one. Deaf students need facilitators rather than enforcers – someone to whom they can come to get help sorting out a problem with their hearing aid as quickly as possible because they want it available when they need it.

Other educational audiology

I spent years as the 'expert' in audiology in the places where I worked. Dictionary definitions of the word 'expert' tend to operate in the area of 'knowledgeable, proficient, professional specialist, skilled authority'. In fact, the expert in audiology in a school tends to be the person who is least afraid of the word. Or in some cases the person who manifests least revulsion at handling recently worn earmoulds. Given that I recall a student who frequently left his hearing aids lying around, and who when he reappeared to claim one would check that it was his not by the serial number, but by sniffing the mould, I understand why some people take this attitude. But be brave. This is a topic about which we must all be prepared to think.

Audiology in schools consists of three areas. The first is dealing with hearing aids and similar technology. This is dealt with in the preceding section. Teachers of KS2 and below (4–11 years) need to check aids and R/T constantly. By KS3 (11–14 years) students should be more independent and responsible, particularly with regard to their personal aids. But checking R/T remains very much a ToD's job, as does ensuring the student has everything switched on. I offer the following two statistics without comment: 2 million people in Britain have hearing aids; 1.4 million people in Britain use hearing aids.

Even if you know that an item of equipment has recently been checked, bear in mind how quickly things can change. The reddest my face has ever been is when a student in lesson 1 complained that his radio aid, which I had checked at the start of the day and found to be perfect, was not working. Annoyed at this obvious attempt to put off the start of work, I made no attempt to check it again, simply taking it into my cupboard, waiting a few moments and then returning it to him with the lying assurance that I had fixed it. He tried it, and again claimed it wasn't working. I began to get annoyed at his awkwardness, and insisted that it was working perfectly. He insisted it wasn't – and to add some credence to his claim, produced the battery from his pocket!

An important, and often neglected, area is the Health and Safety implications of cochlear implants. Unless they are given the information they need, it is likely that many teachers will either never give it a thought, or, in the case of some PE staff, be so terrified that they ban implantees from everything except tiddlywinks (for which they are required to wear a scrum-cap). In reality, the in-school problems are relatively few: Van Der Graaf generators are a total no-no; and other static electricity experiments require removing the processor. For sport, only rugby is likely to be on the list of contact sports that are proscribed (kick-boxing and ice hockey not usually making the average school syllabus); football and other 'vigorous' sports can be played in a scrum-cap.

It is the more unusual aspects of school life, for example, school trips involving passing through airport security scans, where staff need advance warning and reminding again just beforehand! High-speed fairground rides are not recommended for implantees – but they are not forbidden. I personally would ensure that parents get both halves of that advice when they sign up for a school trip.

Most importantly, anyone who might be responsible for taking an implanted student to hospital needs to be aware of the importance of pointing out to medical staff at every stage that they are dealing with an implantee who cannot, for example, be given an MRI scan. This is particularly important if the student does not wear a Medicalert tag – and most don't.

To ensure your information is up to date it pays to regularly check the advice given at www.bcig.org.uk/site/professional/default.htm which offers regularly updated advice to implantees on all aspects of safety relating to their equipment, not merely in school.

The second area of audiology is an understanding of the causes of deafness and their implication for the Deaf person.

Much of this has been dealt with in the Introduction. But one thing not mentioned there is the question of syndromic conditions and their implications.

My favourite website, and I speak here in my capacity as a nerd, lists 324 different causes of sensory-neural deafness. When my publisher suggested I 'up the word count' of this book, I felt sorely tempted to list them all, but instead I take pity on you, dear reader, and simply give you the web address www.wrongdiagnosis.com/d/deafness/intro.htm. Of course, not all of these are syndromes, but many are.

We need to keep other teachers (as well as ourselves) informed of what other symptoms beside deafness may be expected in a student as a result of their having a particular syndrome, if it is likely to have an impact on their general health, their behaviour or their capacity for learning. Usher's (deafness accompanied by later onset of retinitis pigmentosa) is a prime example, given that the increase in visual impairment is likely to occur during the student's secondary school career. If one does not realize the eventual implications of this, one faces the danger that by the time the decline is noticed there has to be a mad rush to set in place the extra support that is required. Because of the late onset of the visual impairment, it is also vitally important that we both advise the students themselves and ensure access to counselling.

My experience is that the best source of information on syndromes often comes not from the medical websites but from those run by parental support groups, who have first-hand experience of the day-to-day realities.

In the case of dominant genetic cases you will get many clues, and hopefully understanding and advice, from the carrier parent. But bear in mind that the severity of the condition varies a great deal between generations. Slight traits in the parent may be major in the child, and vice versa. Indeed, in the case of all syndromes, you need to be aware that not every recorded symptom will emerge significantly in every case.

The third area of audiology is that of monitoring the Deaf student's hearing. It is here where we should come into our own. However, Health and Safety regulations, or perhaps more accurately the paranoiac fear which comes upon schools/ Local Education Authorities (LEAs) of being sued, increasingly circumscribe what can be done.

If you have been trained for taking impressions for ear- moulds, bear in mind that there is often now an expectation, whether written or not, that your competence to do so should be retested and recertified regularly – probably annually.

One of the most useful things that ToDs were able to do in the past was tympanography. In my experience, this is rarely done at regular medical examinations unless there is a per- ceived problem. Yet it provides a vital baseline context within which to examine the Pure Tone audiograms. For example, without it we have no secure way of knowing whether a change in the Pure Tone results are of long-term significance or merely a result of a change in the conductive overlay. And if it is the latter, and the change is for the worse, we are in a position to look for early remediation.

Looking in the ear with an otoscope might be considered invasive and hence a possible assault even if nothing actually goes wrong during the examination. Other than in emergen- cies, it would probably be considered safest to have written parental permission in advance. Even for something as simple as a hearing test we have to consider the question: what if we miss something in testing or examination? By the act of having done the test/examination have we made ourselves liable for a claim of negligence?

But what will happen if we don't intervene? In theory, of course, we cover our backs by putting in writing that the student needs to see their GP or attend the appropriate hospital department. But all too often parents will fail to respond; and all too often the students who miss out are the ones who are most in need.

Irrespective of the Health and Safety implications, there seems to be a trend now for saying that the best place for testing and examination is the hospital and not the school, and that the medical staff and not ToDs are the best people to conduct them. I freely admit that acoustic conditions may be better controlled, and certainly more consistent, in a purpose-built hospital room; but I still believe that our familiarity with the student, the rapport that we have with them, and the confidence they have in us constitute a distinct advantage when conducting tests which the students often dislike and are easily bored by. It is not part of my remit to criticize the medical services, but I well recall an occasion when a member of them with no signing ability turned up to do eye tests. By the time we found out what was going on and sent out a signer to help, she was well into the job, entirely accurately, in her own estimation, interpreting the grunts that the students were making as readings from the ophthalmic chart. We might even have believed her had she not just passed one student on both eyes: the good eye and the glass eye.

Irrespective of what we actually do ourselves in this field, we certainly have a major responsibility for keeping accurate, accessible and usable audiological records; more importantly still, we have the responsibility to know how to usefully interpret them; and that is far more than a parroting of formulae. The threshold for profound deafness is 95 dB. I worked under a member of staff who frequently classified students with a loss of 85–90 dB as profound rather than severe. I finally questioned him about this, and he replied that the testing procedures were hardly so accurate as to be precise within 5 dBs and so we can for all practical purposes say that the threshold is actually 90 dB. I conceded that as reasonable, but persisted that he was also including students registering as high as 85 dB. He looked at me pityingly and explained, as if to a simpleton, 'Surely you know enough Maths to realize that 85 rounds up to 90? And as we have just agreed, 90 is the threshold!' However, before I could open my mouth and argue statistically, he made a weighty and insightful point: 'The truth is that most 85s function as profound.' In this I am sure he was correct. As students get older and cannier and better at concentrating, they may improve their audiogram performance. That does not mean their day-to-day hearing performance also improves.

For convenience, I append a few pieces of factual information which anyone working with the Deaf might find useful in answering questions, or in making a point from time to time. Don't, by the way, spend time going round the National Health Service websites for statistics on Deafness on the assumption that you will thereby be at the cutting edge. A lot of their sites use the figures from RNID – so try there first!

The statistic that is generally regarded as the most memorable is that Deaf children (i.e. with a significant hearing loss in the moderate to profound range) are approximately 1 in 1,000. Other ways of looking at the same statistic are that 840 such babies are born each year in the United Kingdom. That would make 12,000 up to the age of 15, whereas the actual number is nearer 20,000, the remainder being those who lose their hearing after birth, whether permanently or who at any given time are suffering from significant conductive problems.

Once we begin to take the elderly into account, in total, there are close to 700,000 people with severe or profound deafness alone. The number of BSL users is probably not much greater than 50,000.

A very popular question is: What do different sounds represent in terms of dBs? This composite list is as good as any.

10 Breathing
20 Whispering
45 Quiet house
60 Normal conversation
70 Vacuum cleaner
85 Heavy traffic
100 Motorcycle
110 Pneumatic drill
120 Live rock music
140 Jet engine at 100 feet
155 Gunshot at 1 foot
194 Sonic boom close up

The impact of ICT on teaching Deaf students

By far the greatest improvement in the communication, it is probably true to say in the lives, of young Deaf people in recent years has been the rise of the mobile text phone. Not only for the first time do they have a fast, efficient and comprehensive method of medium and long distance communication, but to make it even better, it is also the preferred method of every other child of their age, hearing as well as Deaf; and just to put the icing on the cake, bad spelling is practically obligatory!

We do not have to go back very far to find a time when the only methods of communication over long distances were the telephone (useless for most of the Deaf), the telegram (prohibitively expensive for anything but the most dire emergencies) and the letter, which was incredibly slow: allow a couple of days for delivery; then given the problems that many Deaf have in explaining things clearly in writing, add a few more for the possibility of another letter each way to clear up misunderstandings and ambiguities.

Then came the fax. This was seriously touted for a while as an answer to the problems of Deaf communication, with charity organizations touring Schools for the Deaf giving demonstrations. Of course, unlike letters, the communication was immediate. But although it was invaluable for a few adult Deaf having to get messages to a workplace, it was virtually useless socially, because very few, outside of a business environment, had the rather expensive equipment.

In fact, the communication method of choice for the Deaf became the minicom, a combined keyboard and tiny screen which allowed two users to send text messages to each other down a telephone line. It was portable, in much the same way that before transistor radios appeared we used to regard Bakelite wirelesses as portable – a single person could lift it. But you had to find a telephone with a standard-shaped handset and a power source; and you had to find someone at the other end who had another one – which pretty much confined your phone calls to other Deaf.

The immediate solution to this came with Typetalk, a relay service which typed onto a minicom messages for the Deaf from hearing people who had no such technology themselves, and read aloud their typed replies for the benefit of the hearing participant. It was a slow and slightly cumbersome procedure, but so long as you had access to a minicom it worked; and provided the messages were not so intimate that you did not want even the anonymous and sworn-to-confidentiality Typetalk employee to know! Also, if they registered in advance, the Deaf were entitled to a rebate on phone calls made through Typetalk to compensate for the longer time it took to say everything twice.

All this had to be taught in special Communication Skills lessons, since those who did not have links with the local Deaf community via the Deaf Youth Clubs would probably never even have heard of them.

Then one day came the mobile phone revolution, along with MSN, and suddenly every Deaf student in the school was showing their teachers, including their ICT and Communication Skills teacher, how to use them. They were also showing off to their hearing friends the abbreviations they had used, to the disapproval of some of their teachers, on their minicoms, and which were now de rigeur in the new world of adolescent texting. Furthermore, as most of them now also had computers with internet access at home, they could join in the craze for MSN messaging, again on pretty much equal terms.

I fully expected that Typetalk would disappear overnight. In fact it hasn't. At the end of 2008 they were still relaying 40,000 calls per week. Perhaps the adult Deaf are not so confident with texting. Perhaps they just like the rebate. (There again, in an age when everyone has a watch, the speaking clock still claims 70 million calls a year – they can't all be really sad people who want someone to talk to them.)

So do we still need to teach the use of minicoms and Typetalk? I think, in those two specific cases, it is far less important than it was, but we should nevertheless be trying to expose our students to the full range of communication methods/devices open to them. Options such as palantypists, lip speakers and note takers are ones that they are unlikely to come across in school unless we make positive efforts to bring them in. Nor is it simply a matter of seeing them in action, but of showing them how to make the best use of them. This is especially true of interpreters; many students have experience only of seeing ToDs interpret, and that is quite a different matter.

Twenty years ago, I went to a demonstration of a video phone. As we tried to work out what was being signed by a figure, the jerky and irregular transmission of whose movements made him resemble C3PO having an epileptic fit, we were assured that very soon the technical problems would be ironed out and this would be the 'must have' for all Deaf people. Although some Deaf people make use of webcams on their computers to sign to each other, and mobile phones have the capability to send short videos, we still seem to be little further down this road than we were 20 years ago. Perhaps, like the texting mobile, the resources needed to solve the technical problems will only be made available when it is clear that there is a potential market among the hearing, as well as just the limited world of the Deaf.

Another area where progress has been slower than expected is in the subtitling and signing of television programmes, videos and other similar media such as electronic games. Subtitling, either prepared or typed live, has got very close to 100 per cent on BBC and is strong on the other terrestrial channels. But on channels such as those from the Sky stable, very little progress has been made. The syllogism is clear. The demand for subtitles is far stronger from the hard of hearing than from the Deaf. The age profile of the hard of hearing is predominantly elderly. The elderly are at present less likely than the rest of the population to have non-terrestrial television. Therefore, there is less pressure on Sky and so on to provide subtitles. As the age profile of those with satellite television goes up, as it almost inevitably will as those of us who were brought up on only two channels start to die, we may then see more demand for subtitling.

However, we also have to accept that, for the Deaf with limited language, subtitles can inevitably only be of limited use. It makes no difference what is typed on screen if they cannot understand it, or if it has flashed on to the next sentence before they have worked out what it said, or if they are having to concentrate so hard on reading the subtitles that they do not have time to watch what is happening on the film. It is important to remember this when dealing with videos shown in lessons. Do not sit back and assume that you can have an easy time while the students watch it. All too often, you will need to sign explanations of crucial points because the student will not pick it up from the subtitles.

Another thing that used to appear in Communication Skills lessons was the use of Ceefax and Teletext pages. This was extremely heavy going, since the pages were often difficult to read in terms of the language used (the football scores were an exception) and the lack of illustration, beyond the crudest of cartoons, made them unattractive to children. Although Deaf students might believe that the subtitles on 888 were aimed at them and could occasionally be coaxed into looking at the few pages linked to programmes like *See Hear*, they never came to see Ceefax as being 'their' information service, which is probably just as well given that when analogue broadcasting comes to an end in 2012 it will disappear entirely and be replaced with an internet-based system such as Internet Protocol Television (IPTV).

Nor has there been much progress with signed interpretation of television programmes. The target for BBC and the Deaf Broadcasting Council remains at about 5 per cent. Again, we go back to the problem that the hard of hearing, who have the numbers to achieve some clout, rarely sign and so have no interest in this. Worse, like many of the hearing, they will probably dislike 'open' signing as a distraction and a cluttering of their screen. 'Closed' signing, whether by a real person or by an avatar (cartoon-like model: this requires less memory to transmit, but many Deaf don't like it; they miss out on features like facial expression), on a dedicated 'page' like the present subtitles on 888 is still under research.

Points to consider:

- At what developmental point do Deaf students become able usefully to take their own decisions regarding hearing aids?
- As technology increasingly has 'no user-serviceable parts', will educators become increasingly deskilled in this area?
- If so, what will be the implications for their ability to offer help and advice in audiological matters to students and families?

6

Curriculum Issues

Strategies for improving numeracy standards in Deaf students

'Why are Deaf students so bad at Maths?' is a question I have frequently had to field. My defensive response is to assert that I have taught Deaf students who were very good at Maths. But deep in my heart I know that as a generalization the question is justified.

My accursed interrogator then goes on, 'But surely some areas of Maths, algebra for instance, are ideal for Deaf students because they have virtually no language inherent in them?' It sounds a fair point, yet I know from experience that algebra is actually one of the things they find it most difficult to 'get'. To me, this is the giveaway. I believe that the problem is not in itself one of language. At the heart of the problem lies the fact that what the Deaf find it hardest to cope with is abstraction. Because their primary sense, their primary intake for both language and knowledge, is visual, the concrete they do at once; the abstract takes a lot longer.

If this observation is correct, then to solve the numeracy problem it is vital to look beyond the language question; it is not relevant whether the Maths is being presented in English, in BSL or in Mathematese. But the base that it is being built upon must be as concrete as possible. Practical work should be to the fore; algebra should be very low on our priorities until the groundwork is solid. Fortunately, our Lords and Masters are at last saving us the job of have having to go UDI on this one, by belatedly recognizing the importance of Functional Maths to all students.

Parental involvement in Functional Maths means not just helping with homework, but as an integral aspect of students' home lives. What I am absolutely sure of is that it is fruitless to try to win cooperation in this by herding parents into school and lecturing them for an hour on the importance of Functional Maths. I know no better way of scaring off the numerophobes. Functional Maths will become the New Maths of 40 years ago and, as happened then, a whole generation of parents will abandon trying to help their children with Maths because 'we don't understand this New Maths'. It is far better to entice them into school with some non-mathematical event, and give them a quick 10 minutes on how to involve children in everything from shopping to calculating how many ice creams they could have bought with the money Mother has just found out that Father has been spending on porn sites. Above all they need to be seen in the home as facilitators not enforcers.

One other thing our students now have in their favour is that we seem to be coming closer to the day when the battle between the advocates of free use of calculators and those who feel it important that students be able to carve the calculations on their cave walls 'just in case' may be resolved in favour of the former. But the corollary of this is that appreciating that calculator skills are distinct, need to be taught, and are not easy. Hands up all those teachers who have seen students in GCSE exams trying to do algebra on a calculator by using the multiplication sign as an x! I rest my case.

Enjoyment and understanding are closely linked. Just as in an earlier chapter I pointed out the importance of raising the status of writing, so the status of success in Maths is important. The idea that Maths skills are to be found only in swots and nerds burns strongly, but what fires it is often not the prejudices of fellow students so much as those of the adults they meet.

We cannot stop their parents saying 'Oh, never mind. I could never do Maths either.' But we *can* legislate against staff in school saying it – however true one suspects the remark might be! We can also make sure that the display boards in the prime sites for public attention sometimes carry Maths instead of always poetry and artwork.

It is not uncommon to hear some Maths teachers talking about the need for Numeracy Across the Curriculum to be on a par with Literacy Across the Curriculum. Although I am happy to stand by the old watchword of ToDs that 'Every lesson is a language lesson', the idea of trying to make every lesson a Maths lesson terrifies me – and what is more, terrifies me in my persona as a Maths teacher. I just know that if six non-Maths specialists start to introduce calculations into their lessons, whatever they have been told, there will be seven different methods used. And the questions asked will be as fascinating as 'So if Anne of Bohemia was born in 1366 and died in 1394, how old was she when she died?' Where there is real scope for cross curricular work is specifically in ICT and Science where the use of Maths forms a natural part of certain topics – whether spreadsheets or motion. As to the rest, I will be content if all staff will use a common system of signs for numbers and processes.

Using Deaf role models in teaching

I have made the point elsewhere that teachers take their examples from among the people they are familiar with; and almost invariably these will be hearing. Even if a music teacher mentions Beethoven, it will need to be a good day before they comment that he was Deaf, and spent much of his time biting on a stick which went into his piano, so that he could get some of the sound to his brain via the skull, thus cutting out the damaged ossicular chain in his middle ear. A more Deaf-conscious music teacher might quote Evelyn Glennie; one with different musical priorities might mention Pete Townshend going deaf. There is a website, www.deafwiki.org, dedicated to famous Deaf people, which you may care to try, but it is limited in what it has, and what it has is mainly American.

Douglas Tilden might prove an interesting subject for a Deaf student needing to look at the work of an individual artist. He was born Deaf and went on to become a 'name' sculptor. But he was not exactly in the league of Brancusi or Epstein, so Art teachers are unlikely to come up with his name unless they have been primed. Goya, on the other hand, is very likely to crop up in an Art lesson, but few Art teachers will know that he was Deaf from his early 40s.

In Science, there is a strong chance that the name of Thomas Edison, Deaf since his school days, will turn up. Likewise Alexander Graham Bell who, though not deaf himself, had a Deaf wife and mother and invented the telephone as an accidental result of trying to create an improved hearing aid for them: definitely not, as some have suggested, just to annoy them because they couldn't use it.

In ICT, we might mention Vinton Cerf designer of Arpanet and hence founding father of the internet. We don't really get the expression Cerfing the Net from him, but hey, if it's a peg to hang the information from . . . !

For PE, one might expect that Deaf sportsmen would be a little thicker on the ground, but they are only marginally so. Gertrude Ederle was the first woman to swim the Channel. There have been occasional professional sportsmen who were Deaf, but the majority are in American sports and even if you teach in the heart of Arsenal-land I doubt if the name

Cliff Bastin means very much today. Given that there are ToDs now working in schools who were not born when Lester Piggott won his last Derby on Teenoso, it might be just as convenient to use Deafy Morris as an example of a Deaf sportsman. Jack Morris rode the winners of the 1873 Thousand Guineas and the 1875 Derby. He almost lost the Derby because he failed to hear the second horse coming up very close behind him or the shouts of spectators trying to warn him. He died in poverty in a cellar, addicted to drink. Most jockeys of his period did! At least Morris' deafness was unequivocal; no one was quite so sure of Piggott. After winning a race he, whether accidentally or deliberately, forgot to give the usual tip from his winnings to the stable lad who had looked after the winning horse. The following week the lad saw him and said, 'Mr Piggott, can I have a quid for that winner last week?' Piggott looked vague and said, 'Sorry, son. I can't hear you. You're on my deafest side.' The lad went round to his left side and asked, 'Mr Piggott, can I have a couple of quid for that winner last week?' Piggott replied, 'Sorry, son. Still can't hear you. Try the one quid ear again.'

In History, the emperor Hadrian went deaf. Goodness knows what he thought he was agreeing to when he told his generals they could build a wall across Britain!

The French poet Ronsard was Deaf but his early dialect of French means he is unlikely to be much quoted in Modern Languages, even if your students are not exempted from that subject. Oliver Heaviside worked on advances in differential equations and vector analysis – and the chances of those cropping up in GCSE Maths are pretty remote; though probably not as remote as a Geography lesson on the 250 counties of the State of Texas, one of which is Deaf Smith County, named after the Texan Independence hero Erastus Smith.

What one comes down to is that very few Deaf people were world leaders in their field. Juliette Gordon Low, who was America's equivalent of Lady Olave Baden Powell, was deaf in one ear as a result of a grain of rice getting stuck in it, after being thrown at a wedding. Complications set in!

There are a number of Deaf whom our students should perhaps learn about because they are people whose significance as figures really only manifests itself within the Deaf world. Ferdinand Berthier set up the first international organization of the Deaf. Pierre Desloges was the first Deaf person to have his books published – political works during the French Revolution. L'Epee, Clerc, the Gallaudets and King Jordan have all had an important role in Deaf education. None of these are British. A few years ago one would have confidently said that every Deaf student should be made aware of Jack Ashley, but such is the temporary nature of fame that I'm no longer sure there would be much point to it.

All of this does however return us to the point I made in an earlier chapter – that there is a desperate need for a window in Deaf students' timetables for Deaf Culture as a separate subject.

I have left until last the question of English Literature and Deaf writers, because the question here is more complex than in the case of other subjects. There is a complexity in that there are two distinct ideas involved: writings about Deaf characters (irrespective of whether or not the author is Deaf) and writings by Deaf authors (irrespective of whether or not any of the characters described are Deaf); although authors tending to write from their own experience, it is quite likely that where the author is Deaf so will be at least some of the characters.

From Smollett's *Peregrine Pickle* and Walter Scott's *Talisman,* via Wilkie Collins' *Hide and Seek,* to Faulkner's *Mansion* and

Lee's *To Kill a Mocking Bird* there are classic novels with Deaf characters; but many are minor and these are hardly works that will receive much coverage in English lessons. Modern novels by 'big name' authors such as *The Silent World of Nicholas Quinn* by Colin Dexter or *For the Sake of Elena* by Elizabeth George, although they might give hearing people an interesting insight into attitudes both of and towards the Deaf, are unlikely to be read by students. Deaf novelists of any reputation are rare and confined to the United States (e.g. Stevie Platt).

The result of all this is that once again we are looking for sources that lie outside the mainstream of literature, and certainly will not appear in most mainstream English lessons. So if we research in this area, it is less likely that we will be doing it to inform another teacher, as to inform and encourage the student to extend their reading. As a starting point, I recommend www.myshelf.com/deaf/characters.htm albeit it is strongly American. Also, given what we know about Deaf students' reading ages, I suggest the *7–12* section is a better bet than the *Teen/Young Adult* section for all but our best readers.

A final point regarding literature is that surely every Deaf student should realize that Deaf poetry exists – but here again we face two separate manifestations. The first is the written textual poetry produced by Deaf writers. Trawling the internet will produce any number of examples, and, as with hearing poetry, the fact that it is on the internet is no guarantee of its quality. But they will suffice at least to get Deaf students involved in poetry and can equally well be used by teachers with mainstream classes as general examples. As a starting point, try http://gupress.gallaudet.edu/excerpts/DAP.html. The second manifestation, however, is Deaf poetry in pure BSL with no written form possible, or at least not desirable, being no more than a crude translation. And since it cannot be satisfactorily rendered as text, it will never 'crop up' in mainstream English lessons. We therefore need to find for our students visual recordings of the work of people such as Dorothy Miles.

All that I have said in this section can be summarized under the heading of Giving Students Deaf Role Models. In a multicultural society you have to bear in mind that any given students may regard themselves as a member of an ethnic group as strongly as they identify with the Deaf community. If you have found difficulty in finding a Deaf role model for Science, you might care to reflect on the difficulty of finding a Deaf Vietnamese/Somali/Inuit role model for the same subject. But what you can, indeed must, do is look for ethnic Deaf role models appropriate to your students that you can use to inspire them in a general fashion.

Careers education

The sabre-toothed curriculum was a concept much talked about in the 1970s. I imagine that in the twenty-first century it has itself become extinct, and will require explanation. The story goes like this:

Once upon a time people lived in caves. Survival depended on the tribe's ability to hunt the woolly mammoth on which they relied for food and clothing, and to trap the sabre-toothed tiger which threatened their safety. It was a tough life, and a close-run thing, which required the active participation of every man, woman and child. But they got better at it. They perfected techniques which made them more efficient, and their expeditions more reliable. Women and children no longer had to take part. Eventually even the older men were no longer required. Instead they could stay in the cave and teach the children, who were no longer seeing the systems in action, the theory of how to hunt woolly mammoths and trap sabre-toothed tigers. The system became so efficient that soon the mammoth and the sabre-toothed tiger were extinct. Instead, they hunted the wild ox and trapped their new enemy, the wolf. But back in the cave the old men, reluctant to change their lesson plans, continued to teach only mammoth hunting and tiger trapping. When they were criticized for being out of date they replied that they were teaching generic skills that were applicable to any situation and any animal.

I don't suppose any of us are so sabre-toothed in our approach that we are still literally teaching baking, printing and cobbling, which a 100 years ago were the trades that most (male) Deaf students went into. But there is always a danger that we do not react quickly enough to see how advances in technology can extend the range of possible careers for students.

At the same time it is important to remain realistic; technology may sweep away many of the problems of communication. But they do not solve the problem of low literacy levels. In recent years there have emerged certain predictive surveys, supposedly normed on Deaf people, aimed at helping students to choose careers. Some of the suggestions have gone into the realms of fantasy in the eyes of those who know the students concerned.

I remember in the days before I began to work with the Deaf, teaching English to a child who clearly had tremendous difficulties with basic literacy. Whenever careers were discussed he steadfastly made the same choice: he was going to be a journalist. I never wanted to crush ambition, but it always seemed both a bizarre and a wholly unrealizable choice for the individual concerned. (In those days, journalists were still expected to be able to write in decent English.) Eventually at a parents' evening I risked broaching it with his mother. 'Oh, that!' she replied.

'When he was at Primary School he had a letter printed on the Children's Page of the *Hartlepool Mail*. His Uncle told him he'd have to be a journalist when he grew up.'

There is a danger that these programmes have become the kindly, amusing uncles. A child shows an interest in drawing. Career = Architect.

One does not want to create a ghetto mentality, but in looking for potential careers one needs to balance aspiration with reality. Part of that reality lies with the conservatism of employers, and in many cases their lack of experience of the Deaf. In trying to overcome this, our greatest enemy is likely to be the great god Health'n'safety. For every step that the law takes to ensure that disabled people are not discriminated against, 'Injury Lawyers 4 Compo' take two steps in the other direction to scare employers into calculating what an accident might cost them. And this starts at the very beginning with trying to get Deaf students the simplest work experience placement. Furthermore, it offers employers who are really more insecure about other aspects, such as communication and whether the Deaf will frighten the horses, something to hide behind. If they are genuinely worried about communication, that is fine, because it is not too difficult to show them how modern technology, and modern legislation offering money to solve communication problems, can resolve these difficulties.

One perhaps returns to the bakers and printers. Why were they once the career choice of so many Deaf? It may be that initially they were found to be trades where communication was less important than concentration. But once it became established, employers became used to them, and the Deaf were happy to work in areas where there were already a number of others with whom they could communicate. This may have suited a time when patterns of employment remained unchanged over decades, if not centuries, but cannot be our guiding principle now.

We need to look for opportunities. It may sound a terrible thing to suggest, but given equal employment opportunity legislation, particularly the Disability Discrimination Act of 2005, we are moving into a situation where token Deaf may be in heavy demand – be it literally to tick a box, to allow firms to promote themselves locally as a caring company or to have the convenience of having someone on site who can communicate effectively if a Deaf customer comes in. Many shops, clubs and so on found a lucrative niche market catering to the pink pound. I'm sure many can be persuaded that the Deaf Pound is theirs for the taking if they take on some Deaf employees to make the place Deaf friendly.

Points to consider:

- Is Maths in any sense an extra language for Deaf students? To what extent is progress in it supported or limited by their progress in their other language(s)?
- Do the constraints on learning Maths outlined here apply to any other academic subjects?
- Is it reasonable to expect hearing students to have lessons based on figures who have never made a significant impact outside the Deaf community?

7

Professional Cooperation

Working with other teachers

In the 1960s there was a radio comedy programme called *The Men from the Ministry*; it was a forerunner of the later and much funnier *Yes Minister*. In it there was an imaginary civil service department called General Assistance which could be called in by any specialist department to clean up their mess 'with hilarious results' – that is, with complete cock-ups.

There are times when I suspect that ToDs and LSAs/CSWs have been drafted into that department. They are the answer to some of the teachers' prayers – even though in some cases what they were actually praying for may have been for support staff who were younger, more glamorous and of a different sex. In a classroom teeming with recalcitrant teenagers, half of them with special needs that are only dimly or tentatively acknowledged, they are an extra pair of hands.

I do not believe that there is a single model of cooperation which will fit all scenarios, because there are too many variables. Actually there are four variables.

First, there are the Deaf students. They of course vary in the level and intensity of help that they require. Some will require the undivided attention of a member of the support staff and almost constant help for the whole of the lesson. Many need help only to interpret what the teacher vouchsafes to the whole class, and then to be available to help with problems, either from the LSA, or if the problem is a profound one, interpreting a solution from the expert. Some like an LSA sitting with them, just in case. Others would prefer to be like the rest of the class and not have a teacher attached to their neck like a signing albatross.

If you are an LSA, provided you know you can trust them to call you as soon as they need you, there is then no reason not to help others. But return regularly to make sure that (a) they are working (b) they are not going down completely the wrong road and (c) you can watch and note how they are developing.

Second, there is the class teacher. Although I have given the impression that they are all crying out for help with the class, you will find a few who feel that the last thing they want is another adult in the room; and if they have to be there they had better sit quietly in the corner and not start interfering with *their* class. Their reasons may vary from those who doubt the LSA's expertise in their subject, to those who doubt their own and don't want to risk being corrected, and from those who are afraid the support staff will be more popular with the students than they are to those who believe that the support staff will show them up by being tougher with the students than they are – and then report them for their softness.

This is basically just a lesson on how to be diplomatic. Don't point out mistakes in front of the class the first time. Go up at the end and point it out quietly. If at the start of the next lesson they begin by saying, 'Last time I said *x*, but Mrs Y has pointed out that actually it's *z*' you will know you have carte blanche to intervene in future. When it is a matter of helping students, try to decide whether the teacher is particularly interested in the exact nature of students' problems. Some staff are highly diagnostic, and really want to know what a student is having problems with, so they can track their progress and 'inform their future teaching'. Others don't mind who shows them how to do something, as long as someone does. Start with a pupil nearby, and if the teacher doesn't come over to see what's wrong you can work outwards.

Third, there are the hearing students. By and large, hearing students are not hostile to being helped and one adult is as good as another. It is only in disciplinary matters that they are more likely to take the view, 'You can't tell me what to do. You're not my teacher,' or indeed its close friend, 'You can't tell me what to do. You're not my dad.'

The last variable of course is you. You may not feel confident enough with the content of the lesson to be active in sorting out other students' problems in case it turns out to be something you can't answer. I usually find the question 'Is it something simple or do you need the expert teacher?' does well for the self-image of everyone involved.

But whatever view you take about helping with the hearing students, you need to firmly establish your right to 'help' the other teachers by giving advice and correcting bad practice in regard to the Deaf. Correcting them is helping them even though they may not appreciate it as such. But again, be subtle, be diplomatic. Make 'suggestions' at the end of the lesson, rather than interrupting them in full flow. Go over and make points quietly at the desk rather than shouting at them from where you are sitting.

Finally, if all else fails and you believe, whether because of poor classroom management or because the lesson is pitched at an inappropriate level, they are learning nothing, take them out diplomatically. Diplomacy as you know is the art of lying for your country. So lie: 'I think there's something here they haven't met before, so I'm just going to take them out for a bit and see if I can get them up to speed on that.' (Nor will it always be a lie. Often, even with the best of teachers, that is exactly what you will need to do.) If the problem persists, then of course a collective decision, or at least one approved by your line manager, will need to be made as to whether you stay out on a permanent basis.

Learning support assistants

(Please note that in this section, as indeed throughout the book, I have used the term LSA to indicate a person who works in a supporting role with Deaf students, irrespective of whether or not they are acting as, or hold the qualification for, CSWs.)

There is a famous photograph of a notice of correction put up at Lord's cricket ground in 1961, for the attention of all those spectators who had bought the official scorecard. It reads 'For F. J. Titmus, please read Titmus F. J.'. In those days there existed the strictest possible division between amateurs and professionals. The amateurs had their own separate changing room, nearly always supplied the team captain, were put up overnight at the best hotels and sometimes even had their own gate onto the field. Above all, their initials preceded their surname. Or they had a title, as the professional Tom Graveney found to his cost when he dared to congratulate an amateur team-mate on scoring a century with 'Well done, David'; his captain screamed at him angrily 'That's Mr Shepherd to you, Graveney!'

When I first began teaching the Deaf, ToDs and LSAs were separated by a division only slightly less strict. In particular, signing of academic subjects was confined entirely to ToDs, except in the direst of temporary emergencies, and to contemplate any other scenario was seen as dilutionism – a term coined during World War II for the use of unqualified workers to do the job of skilled men who had gone into the army.

Increasingly, this has ceased to be the case. This has happened partly, but only partly, as a result of a general trend since the start of the Millennium for using LSAs in mainstream schools to cover for, rather than simply support, teachers. In the specific case of mainstream schools with Deaf students, one of the problems is that the (hearing) management, who hold the purse-strings, may not understand the differences between a ToD waving their arms about and an LSA doing the same. What they do understand is that the latter is considerably cheaper.

In terms of interpreting, there are two problems. The first is that although an LSA is unlikely to have too much trouble interpreting from scratch, since if the mainstream teacher's explanation is to be comprehensible to the students, it will surely be comprehensible to the LSA, this may not be the case if the lesson takes for granted knowledge from an earlier lesson, if that particular LSA was not interpreting the previous lesson. In my experience LSAs tend to have a specialist subject (if they do not, it should be the responsibility of the school, with active support from the ToDs, to help them gain a speciality, looking both at in-service training and consistency of timetabling). But their specialist knowledge is unlikely to be as deep as that of the ToD with a specialism in the same subject, and the ToD is also likely to have a wider range of knowledge outside their speciality.

The second problem is that, as I have said before in a different context, although ToDs may blithely speak of what they do as interpreting, they are in fact not interpreters: they are teachers operating within the confines of what the mainstream teacher is teaching to the hearing students. It is by no means inevitable that they will choose to present that material in the same way, much less in the same words, as the mainstream teacher. Often they will go into a separate teaching mode, using different examples, adding extra information, filling gaps in the students' knowledge and so on. This is not something that can be demanded of an LSA, though I would be the first to admit that many of them can do this, and do it well.

In other situations, however, the LSA may be working with a ToD, and directly under their control, perhaps with a discretely taught Deaf group. In this circumstance, the ToD must be careful not to fall into the hypocrisy of using them in a way that would be objectionable if others employed it – which is to say, as dogs-bodies. I will not go so far as to say they should never be employed creating learning resources, especially if they enjoy it and have a flair for it; but I will say that I have yet to meet an LSA who enjoys, much less has a flair for, standing next to a photocopier for long periods of time! Most of the time they should be assisting a student's learning by working with them. If a ToD does not have a student in the group who would benefit more than the others from individual attention then (a) they are very lucky and (b) they could probably donate their LSA to someone who does have such a student. Although a ToD can, and often should, alter strategy in the course of a lesson, depending on what unexpected problems are thrown up, they should at least start by giving the LSA a clear, specific and prepared plan of whom to work with and what to do with them, until further instruction.

Finally come the situations when the LSA is required to work alone with a student or a small group. Occasionally they may choose to remove a group from the mainstream class because a particular lesson or topic needs to be taught in a different way from that being used with the hearing majority. But if this is more than a temporary problem it needs to be resolved by a responsible ToD, preferably in consultation with the mainstream teacher and their head of department.

If they are to be used as reader/signer or amanuensis (or even simply invigilator) for public examinations they need to be given very specific instructions – I would prefer to say 'training' – to ensure that they understand and meet the ethical criteria that need to be exercised in this area.

If a ToD wishes them to work alone with individuals or pairs of students from the ToD's own group they need to be presented with a very clear plan of what to do, an explanation of why they are doing it and, equally important, the resources with which to do it. What, however, is often ignored is that they should be presented with more than a single plan. ToDs continually amend their lesson strategies according to how unsuccessfully (and even occasionally how well) it is going. LSAs need to be given at least some outline strategies for what to do if certain difficulties, which can hopefully be anticipated from previous experience, should crop up.

If they are used in this way, bear in mind that the statutory responsibility for monitoring the student's progress and ultimately reporting it does not pass from the ToD's shoulders. Therefore, there needs to be in place a full and accurate system of record keeping; and it is also the ToD's responsibility to ensure that the LSA has the time to do the recording in quiet and leisurely circumstances rather than on the hoof to the next lesson.

Parents, carers and other practitioners

This section will win me few friends, and may well cost me any that I already have; but I do not see how a book of bland platitudes will serve the next generation of our profession.

I once wrote an article in an obscure educational journal about children with special needs (MLD rather than Deaf), but who were well-behaved, who ended up in mainstream classes in which they were wholly unable to cope, as a result of dinner parties! I argued that their middle-class parents, at dinner parties, did not want to admit to their friends that little Peter was at That Place Down The Road (i.e. the Special School) but was of course at the local comprehensive school where he was 'doing very well; in fact he's getting a prize next week at speech day'. The prize was actually a certificate for good attendance and/or good behaviour, but no one at the party would be so gauche as to ask questions about that. So they pulled every string to get their children into mainstream, often at the expense of the child's education, since they would learn nothing there. And teachers connived with it because they knew that the special schools were bursting at the seams with children who were probably a little more able than Peter but displayed far more behavioural problems; why rock the boat and risk a bad swap?

All too often parents of Deaf children have made the same choice. Many will say that they want their Deaf children in mainstream because they have to live in a hearing world. So they do. But schools don't resemble the 'real world' in a lot of other ways. If anything, school is a way of bringing up children so that when they leave they can cope with the world outside school. The crucial point is therefore not how closely the school resembles the post-school world, but how well it prepares students for it by the time they have to join it.

The truth is that most parents have experience of mainstream education. Very few have experience of special education. It is therefore more comfortable for many of them to see their children in mainstream. The danger is that having children in mainstream can blind parents to the difficulties, particularly the language difficulties, that the child is subject to, and fuel unrealistic expectations.

The other problem parents are the Try Anythings. Or perhaps more accurately the Try Everythings. Every fortnight they Google the words 'Deaf' and 'breakthrough'. Whatever comes up, they demand it from the school or the Health Authority. I have seen parents disappear on a weekend course on Cued Speech and return not only fully intending to use it themselves with the child but apparently expecting the school, without a single Cued Speech user, to do the same. The unplanned and piecemeal nature of this attitude more or less guarantees failure, no matter how good the idea may be in itself.

It is easy for people on the outside to say they are still in denial. Staff in school are paid a lot of money to deal with problems in which they do not have the parents' deep emotional investment. And they get to send the children home at 4 o'clock. But while being sympathetic, they need to remain detached, and use that detachment positively.

Nowhere is this better illustrated than in the case of cochlear implants. No sooner had Jack Ashley (deafened late in life) appeared on television saying what a boon his implant was, than parents pushed and pushed for their children to have them, irrespective of how appropriate it was to their case, and well before anyone had looked at their long-term efficacy in pre-lingually deaf children. There was a real moral issue because the claimed need for an early implantation made it impossible to allow the child even an opinion, much less a choice. Some in the Deaf community were appalled in expectation that it might work and the Deaf community would shrivel and die. Perhaps the hearing would have been equally appalled had they known how many of those children would go on to reject those implants.

This is not an attack on cochlear implants. But it is an appeal to all those involved with Deaf students to think carefully about how to respond to medical and technological advance. Parents and medics in tandem are a formidable force. But 'formidable' does not always equal 'right'. It is disturbing how often a single doctor in an area can influence the general trend of what happens to Deaf children – what educational environment they go into as much as what technology they go for. White coats carry more weight than elbow patches.

Educational professionals are not in the position to be able to abolish parents! We cannot, and indeed we should not, ignore them. But successive governments have made it increasingly difficult for professionals to fight parents, and other outside agencies, over issues where professional judgement is required. We must remember that we are the professionals.

> **Points to consider:**
>
> - How far is it reasonable to expect a Special Educational Needs Coordinator who has responsibility for students with a broad range to have knowledge of specifically Deaf problems?
> - If they do not, how far should specialists in Deaf education try to educate them? How far should they expect, as the experts, to be left to go their own way?
> - Does the same apply to relations with a Headteacher or other Senior Manager?
> - By the same token, should educationalists expect to be treated in that way by experts in the field of Speech Therapy or Clinical Audiology?

Afterword – Changing Trends in Deaf Education

When I began teaching the Deaf in the late 1980s, we were very aware of some parts of the history of Deaf Education. In fact, I suppose, we were still living them. However, when Gert McLoughlin published *A History of Deaf Education in England and Wales* in 1987, it was notable that although she had managed to find exact measurements for the frontages of early English schools for the Deaf, she completely failed to mention that large numbers of ToDs had now started using sign, not oral/aural methods of teaching. That was an interesting take on what exactly comprised the history of Deaf Education.

When I was doing my qualification as a ToD, I wrote a History essay on McKay Vernon, the American academic who first revealed the failure of profoundly Deaf students to make progress, academic or emotional, using oral methods; it was returned with the lowest possible pass mark, since I had chosen 'a subject of no relevance to the history of Deaf education'. When we appealed, it went up one grade 'due to the amount of factual information the candidate had amassed' but without any rehabilitation of the validity of Dr Vernon's life work.

Some progress, however, had been made. When I and a group of my contemporaries were observed by outside representatives of British Association of Teachers of the Deaf (BATOD), for the assessment of our practical teaching skills, we were the envy of our predecessors, since we were actually evaluated by signers, while until a year or so earlier the moderators had always been oralists. It never ceases to amaze me how people with no experience of signing are expected, or can hope, to properly judge a signed lesson, whether or not the teacher is voicing; but the habit has still not died out. I have been in a School for the Deaf OFSTEDed by a panel of which only one member had any experience of signing.

We no longer have to argue for our very existence as signers. We are no longer looked on by the profession as being like the four solitary delegates at The 2nd International Congress of Teachers of Deaf Mutes at Milan in 1880 who voted against the opinion of 160 others that 'considering the incontestable superiority of speech over sign in restoring the deaf mute to social life and for giving him greater facility in language the pure oral method should have preference over that of signs in the instruction of the deaf and dumb'. No longer are we expected to beat students we catch signing, nor are Heads expected to beat staff who gesture (oh, all right – order them to sit on their hands while teaching). Yet these things are still within the living memory of a few of our profession.

Indeed, in the eyes of the public we have won. Tell the person on the Clapham omnibus that you teach the Deaf and they will mime a tic-tac man and say, 'You do all that then, do you?' I feel it is a long time since *Mandy* was shown on terrestrial television. Not that I want to claim that public perception is necessarily the benchmark for what we do. I well recall once being asked what my job was, and having told them, being met with a sympathetic look and the words, 'Oh dear. I *am* sorry. That must be really distressing for you.'

So far is oralism nowadays from being all-conquering that my word processor's dictionary refuses to accept the word without a red underline, and suggests that I might mean organism; for 'oralists' it would prefer 'royalists'. The days are long gone when 'signers' would have been queried as potential 'singers'.

Much of this change can be put down to the influence of television and the appearance of signers on it. In reality, of course, much more of the impact of this has been within the signing community itself where signing, which was once a very regional thing, is now rather more cosmopolitan in its outlook. I do not know if it is any longer possible, as I am assured it once was, to guarantee a riot by organizing a bingo session with participants from two different areas and the caller from a third (the numeral signs in different areas never being compatible). One waits to see if the media spread of signing across the world does anything to revive interest in International Sign Language (ISL).

And so our particular wave broke upon the beach of Deaf History. Inevitably, the tide has brought in many more waves, and will continue to do so.

Hot upon the heels of the Sign v Speech debate came the question of whether, if sign is being used, BSL or SSE is the most appropriate format. This began very much as another polarization, with SSEers claiming that BSL could not effectively teach English, and BSLers claiming that SSE failed to teach language, since it was not in itself a real language. Fortunately, this has generally turned out to be much less acrimonious. Some schools have taken deliberate policies that in the same institution it is possible to teach English as a separate subject to BSL users, and BSL to those who have been brought up on English structure. Less formally, in other cases where SSE is the dominant teaching mode, BSL users are brought in as role models and to give experience of the other mode.

Then came the decline in numbers of the Schools for the Deaf and the victory of mainstreaming. I have dealt in another chapter with many of the implications of this in schools where 'bases' of Deaf students exist. But of course many Deaf students within mainstream are more isolated. Those who can cope with occasional peripatetic support have always been with us. But the growth of parent power is increasingly leading to single Deaf students with permanent individual communication support – an expensive option, as well as one which may yet prove that the problems of such students are not simply academic, but also social.

I suspect that many of us felt that cochlear implants were likely to have a major impact on what we did, even if we did not share the fears of those in the Deaf community who saw it as a kind of ethnic cleansing to do away with the Deaf entirely. In reality, it has made little difference to our actual teaching, as opposed to the audiological aspect of our ability, or otherwise, to intervene and fix problems. Much the same can be said for the introduction of digital aids.

And so we look at the present, and its close friend the future. I think the most surprising and certainly the most significant statistic I have come across recently is '*Among severely or profoundly deaf people under 60, 45% have additional disabilities.*' Please read that again, several times if necessary. Of course we have always been aware that there was a higher proportion of additional disabilities among the Deaf, partly as a result of genetic syndromes, partly because traumas which were sufficient to cause deafness were also likely to cause other damage. Nevertheless, many of us thought of ourselves, even if we avoided speaking such an unPC term, as educating 'Normal Deaf'. Increasingly, we are being asked to educate Deaf students with considerable additional problems, which make genuine mainstreaming, as opposed to merely containing them within a mainstream school exceptionally difficult. Where these additional problems are predominantly physical, they can largely be overcome by additional support; but where they are emotional, behavioural or related to learning ability (or combinations thereof) they are much more difficult to resolve.

We also see the use of the Deaf label for students with comparatively low levels of hearing loss. Very often this is seen by schools as a quick fix when it comes to the problems of statementing students who clearly have other learning problems, whether academic or behavioural/emotional: the Deaf label is the most 'objective' and likely to persuade LEAs or management that support is required.

The next stage of this trend, which many of us are now coming to experience, is the teaching of classes with a mixture of Deaf students and those who are hearing but have additional learning problems. As I have suggested elsewhere, I believe that our experience and knowledge of the problems of language acquisition makes us uniquely able not merely to cope with this situation but to make a positive and confident contribution.

List of Abbreviations

BATOD – British Association of Teachers of the Deaf – a professional organization representing Teachers of the Deaf on consultative panels, and advising them on a personal basis. Publishes relevant research articles and so on. But you have to pay.

BSL – British Sign Language. Language of the British Deaf community. A language, not simply a vocabulary; it has its own word order, grammar and so on. Constantly evolving, sometimes while you are actually watching it.

BTE – Behind the Ear – hearing aids that sit snugly behind the pinna of the ear. Unless you got the length of the connecting tube wrong, in which case they waggle in the wind like antennae.

CMV – Cytomegalovirus. Essentially Rubella without spots, though actually it is a form of herpes. They tend to keep quiet about that!

CSW – Communication Support Worker. In some schools an interpreter. In others, a learning support assistant (LSA) with special extra features.

FAQ – Frequently Asked Questions – questions which either (a) are never really asked because the answers are so obvious or (b) are frequently asked because no one can ever give a sensible answer to them.

GCSE – General Certificate of Secondary Education. A public examination at the end of Key Stage 4 (ages 14–16), which we are told each year by experts is too easy for the top 49.5 per cent and too difficult for the bottom 49.5 per cent.

Hz – Hertz – a measure of how high or low a frequency is. Most speech is between 250–4,000 Hz. Once you get much over

10,000, start thinking dog whistles. More usefully, they will also rent you vans.

ICT – Information and Communication Technology. Previously known as Information Technology. Previously known as Computer Studies. Previously known as That Be Witchcraft.

IPTV – Internet Protocol Television – A newfangled method of giving access to Web pages using a television signal. Television is a newfangled form of radio with pictures.

ISL – International Sign Language – Previously known as Gestuno. Sometimes used at international conferences. It is the exact equivalent of Esperanto in that you can go to any country in the world and find people there who don't use it.

ITA – Initial Teaching Alphabet – An alphabet which, when you read or write in it, has no irregular sounds – but cheats slightly by having 44 letters including æ, 3 and the ever popular ω, as well as others that I cannot reproduce on my computer without a special font or a serious virus.

ITE – In the Ear – miniaturized hearing aids that fit snugly and quietly in the ear canal, until they don't fit snugly any more, at which point they don't fit quietly either.

KS (1/2/3/4) – Key Stage – The four divisions of compulsory school age (1 = Y1 – 2, 2 = Y3 – 6, 3 = Y7 – 9, 4 = Y10 – 11) at the end of each of which students are assessed. Or not.

LEA – Local Education Authority. A function of elected local councils that run all the schools in the area except for all the ones which government initiatives have taken away and put into the hands of unelected bodies.

LSA – Learning Support Assistant. Someone who works as hard as we teachers do, for half our money.

OFSTED – Office for Standards in Education. An organization responsible for inspecting schools, evaluation of standards, teacher suicides and so on.

QCA – Qualifications and Curriculum Authority – a group of serious educationalists who spend 364 days a year guarding and improving the quality of public examinations, and one day a year giving the contract for marking them to ETS Europe. Now renamed the QCDA.

RNID – Royal National Institute for the Deaf. A charity aimed at helping Deaf people and supporting their families. In recent years they have increased the number of Deaf people employed there and their involvement of the Deaf community. But there is a generation of Deaf who still point out accusingly that they are 'for the Deaf' and not 'of the Deaf'.

R/T – Radio Telemetry. Radio Hearing Aid systems, which attempt to cut out background noise by broadcasting short wave radio transmissions directly from a microphone fixed near the teacher's mouth to the student's hearing aid. I believe this term is also used to describe the system used in Formula One racing cars to transmit complex data at lightning speed, while still sounding like the tannoy on Euston station when they speak down it.

SSE – Sign Supporting English. A method of signing in which BSL signs are administered in English word order to correspond with the lip pattern of someone speaking English. SSE is to BSL roughly what *Carry On Camping* is to hard-core porn.

ToD – Teacher of the Deaf – a harmless drudge who once upon a time was told by a Headteacher that when he/she qualified for that title the world would be their oyster.

Further Information

Books on Education are expected to end with a bibliography which constitutes either

(a) acknowledgement of all the sources from which the author took information; or
(b) an extensive reading list of all the latest works available on the subject in hand.

This book was not (at least consciously) compiled from other people's material so much as from my practical experiences. Nor do I have the time or finance to keep abreast of everything that is published in this field. Consequently, I will attempt nothing comprehensive. Instead, here is a brief list of books which, over the years, I have found particularly helpful or inspiring, and a brief list of websites that rendered me useful collateral information. For a more comprehensive list of books on this subject still in print see www.forestbooks.com.

Ballantyne, J. and Martin J. A. M. (1984), *Deafness*. Edinburgh: Churchill Livingstone.

Fletcher, Lorraine (1987), *Language for Ben*. London: Souvenir Press.

Grant, Brian (1988), *The Quiet Ear*. London: Faber and Faber.

Lane, Harlan (1976), *When the Mind Hears*. New York: Random House.

Montgomery, George ed. (1978), *Of Sound and Mind*. Edinburgh: Scottish Workshop Publications.

Montgomery, George ed. (1981), *Integration and Disintegration of the Deaf in Society*. Edinburgh: Scottish Workshop Publications.

RNID (n.d.), *Effective Inclusion of Deaf Pupils into Mainstream Schools*. London: Royal National Institute for the Deaf.

Sainsbury, Sally (1986), *Deaf Worlds*. London: Hutchinson.

Webster, Alec and Ellwood, John (1985), *The Hearing Impaired Child in the Ordinary School*. London: Croom Helm.

Deafness and Education International (previously *The Journal of the British Association of Teachers of the Deaf*).

Talk (Magazine of The National Deaf Children's Society).

Useful Websites

www.batod.org.uk: *A one-stop resource for information relating to the British Association of Teachers of the Deaf.*

www.deafsign.com: *A guide to signing and deaf awareness.*

www.disabled-world.com/artman/publish/famous-deaf.shtml: *A biographical list of famous men and women with hearing impairments or deafness.*

www.milan1880.com/index.html: *An extensive history of the infamous conference where sign language was effectively forbidden.*

www.myshelf.com/deaf/characters.htm: *Online bibliography listing works of fiction featuring Deaf characters.*

www.ndcs.org.uk: *Homepage of the National Deaf Children's Society.*

www.rnid.org.uk: *Homepage of the Royal National Institute for Deaf People.*

www.wrongdiagnosis.com/d/deafness/intro.htm: *Online diagnostic guide to deafness.*

Index

Also available from Continuum . . .

Supporting Children with Learning Difficulties: Holistic Solutions for Severe, Profound and Multiple Disabilities
Christine Turner

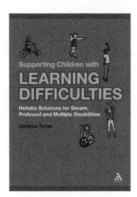

'A comprehensive text suitable for both practitioners and parents. A wealth of strategies are shared'

Edward Sellman, Lecturer in Education, University of Nottingham, UK

How do you teach history to a child who can't remember what they had for dinner? What difference will it make to a child's counting skills if you place the objects in a line? Will breaking down a task into smaller steps help a young person learn how to dress himself?

Christine Turner draws on 25 years' experience of working with learning disabled children and young people to provide an introduction to learning disabilities and the effect they have on the individual and their family. All aspects of learning, from the simplest forms of non-verbal communication to the way ICT can motivate and inspire are explored in this informal guide for anyone wanting to support a child with learning difficulties.

£19.99/$34.95

9781441121776 (PB) / 9781441198792 (PDF) / 9781441167767 (ePub)

www.continuumbooks.com

Supporting Children with Dyslexia – Second Edition

Gary Squires and Sally McKeown

'An enterprising and user-friendly book… It guides the reader through current and changing systems and practices in the maintained sector, and succeeds in its primary aim to provide practical resources for support and intervention.'

Martin Turner, Chartered Educational Psychologist

This expanded and updated second edition focuses on the practical difficulties facing dyslexic pupils every day in the classroom and provides teachers and parents with strategies to support and enable them to access the curriculum with a minimum of fuss and upheaval. The pupil's perspective is also considered, with a section devoted to encouraging children to be positive about themselves and become independent learners.

£24.99/$49.95

9780826434166 (PB) / 9781441174062 (PDF) / 9781441130938 (ePub)

www.continuumbooks.com